GOD'S WEDDING BAND

GOD'S WEDDING BAND

Reflections on the Creation-Evolution Controversy

Norman DeJong

ISBN 1-877607-14-2

To Wilma

My loving wife of more than thirty-two years, who reads and
responds to almost every word I have ever written. For her constant
reminders about Christian love, integrity, kindness, and courage, I
am deeply indebted.

Contents

Foreword: Gary Parker ix

Foreword: Henry Morris xi

Acknowledgements xiii

Introduction. 1

Chap. 1. The Warfare Metaphor 7

Chap. 2. The Real War 15

Chap. 3. What is Science? 25

Chap. 4. The Power of Persuasion 33

Chap. 5. The Problem with Dating. 39

Chap. 6. God's Wedding Band 55

Epilogue. 59

Appendix A: A Case in Point 65

Appendix B: Replies to a Geologist 71

Appendix C: Organizations Formed to React to Evolutionism 87

Notes 91

Bibliography 95

Index. 101

Foreword

WITH liberals looking over their left shoulders at professors prominently identified with Calvinism, it's invigorating to read a Reformed scholar who has his spectacles on correctly—looking at God's world through the light of God's Word, and not the reverse.

Dr. Norman DeJong and I were colleagues at Dordt College before he went to Trinity and I to ICR (Institute for Creation Research). Norm was known then as one who stood firm on the Scriptures and stood up against compromise. He still does. Treating the concepts underlying the major issues, Dr. DeJong uses clear logic and telling examples to show that there is no scientific reason to compromise with evolution, and every Scriptural reason not to compromise.

Leaving other books to refute the detailed obfuscations of "science falsely so-called," Dr. DeJong gets to the heart of the Scriptural principles at hand. In doing so, he helps to restore one of the most important doctrines of all: the perspicacity of Scripture, the foundational truth that God's Word makes wise the simple and enables them to judge "experts" against the yardstick of inerrant—and understandable—revelation. It's my fervent prayer that, in doing so, Dr. DeJong will remove a feeling of confusion and timidity too common among our laity and restore to them the confidence and boldness in Christ to check self-styled "scholarship" against the Scriptures to see whether or not these things be so.

At stake is whether we have the strength to stand on the trustworthiness and timelessness of God's Holy Word.

Dr. Gary E. Parker
Professor of Natural Science
Director of the Florida Creation Science Center
Clearwater Christian College

Foreword

NORMAN DeJong's new book, *God's Wedding Band,* written by
a distinguished educator in the Christian Reformed Church, is a
refreshing antidote to the pro-evolutionary views of many science
professors in that denomination. Although it postulates a supposed
conflict between the Biblical flood and the Ice Age (which was
actually an after-effect of the Flood) and allows for such un-
necessary compromises as the day-age theory and gap theory, it
presents strong evidence against evolution and for the integrity of
God's Word. It should be of real help in the creationist cause, especially in his own denomination.

Henry M. Morris
President
Institute for Creation Research

Acknowledgements

THE life history of a manuscript is known best by its author, but peopled by a number of persons who shaped and molded it over its period of development. Some of those persons will never know how their comments and contributions influenced its final form, for even the author has failed to note the twists and turns of his own thought processes over the four years that this manuscript has been in process.

The genesis of this short book can be traced to a week in early June, 1986. With encouragement from my administrators at Trinity, I was able to attend a week-long conference on "Christianity and the History of Science," sponsored by the Christian College Coalition. Under the leadership of Ronald Numbers and David Lindgren, both of the University of Wisconsin, all of us were challenged to analyze and evaluate the relationships between our Christian faith and our scientific endeavors. To both Lindgren and Numbers I owe a huge debt of gratitude for coercing and cajoling me to reflect long and often about the history of natural science in the context of Christianity.

My response to their efforts was an attempt to put my thoughts in print. The next few months produced four long, tedious chapters which various critics politely acknowledged as being dull, pedantic, and unworthy of publication. Their kind condemnations convinced me to put the manuscript aside. I bear them no malice, but neither will I recite their names or affiliations here.

After almost a year of indolence, I was again spurred to action, this time by Ken Bootsma, my friend and our college president, who prevailed upon me to review and critique *The Fourth Day*, by

Howard Van Til, a professor of astronomy and physics at my alma mater. The ensuing dialogue, correspondence, and debate, both private and public, convinced me that a re-examination of the biblical account of both creation and the Noahic flood was necessary. Having studied Genesis intensively a number of years prior, the research was both revealing and rewarding. Although Howard and I come to Scripture with similar backgrounds, it will be obvious to those who read either this book or his publications that we come to our tasks with different mind-sets and different presuppositions. Although he will probably find much in these pages with which to disagree, it is no secret that my efforts are, at least in part, a response to his. For his willingness to dialogue and debate, a public and hearty thanks. Hopefully out of controversy will come clarity.

Another person who served as a friendly spur to my flagging efforts was John Van Dyk, the managing editor of the *Christian Renewal*. By constantly requesting additional articles for his magazine and then dressing them up with pictures and impressive design, John quietly but effectively challenged me to meet numerous deadlines. For all of that, plus the permit to publish all of those articles in this format, a sincere expression of praise and appreciation.

Along the way there were a host of others. To my brother Les for supplying me with the picture that graces the cover and served to supply the theme for this book. To Burton Rozema, our Academic Dean at Trinity, for his constant encouragement and for his pointed reminders that I, too, could enjoy academic freedom within the bounds of our common Reformed faith. To Mary Lynn Colosimo, Patsy Ruchala, and Harold Van Kley, colleagues at Trinity who found much to endorse and to applaud in these pages. To Bob Boomsma, Lou Sytsma, Gary Van Dyke, and Bob Wolff, all of whom read and wrote reactions to Chapter 6 on "The Nature of Science." To Calvin Hoogendoorn, my pastor and friend, who read much of the early manuscript and offered cogent insight into the nature of the controversy. To Karen Longman of the Christian College Coalition, to Thom Notaro of the Presbyterian and Reformed Pub. Co., and to Jim Weaver of Baker Book House, for their repeated encouragement to continue, even when the initial materials were not worthy of publication. To Ken Ham of the Institute for Creation Research, who graciously gave me permission to use a number of drawings and whose frequent correspondence over many months was a source of inspiration. To all of them I owe a debt of gratitude for sharpening my insights, for giving me their honest reactions, and for making me believe that this work was worth doing.

On the publishing end, a great deal of professional help and advice came from Marshall and Amy Nelson of Redeemer Books. Their insights, suggestions, experience, and editorial skill were immeasurably helpful in producing the top quality products for which they are rapidly becoming noted. In my own office I could not do without the computer skills of Susan Sulicz, who entered, proof-read, revised, and produced the entire manuscript.

Henry M. Morris, President of the Institute for Creation Research, has probably done more than any other person in our generation to keep alive the flame of Biblical creationism. When he consented to write a promotional statement for this book, I was overwhelmed with elation. Though we do not agree on every jot and tittle, his contribution is very meaningful. Being able to stand side by side with him in defense of our Christian faith is a real encouragement and blessing.

A special word of thanks is also due Gary Parker, a former teaching colleague and long-time friend, for writing the Foreword. Gary, having a distinguished record as an author, lecturer, and teacher, has endeared himself to thousands of creationists around the world. His endorsement is deeply appreciated.

Finally, a special thanks to my loving wife of more than thirty-two years, who reads and responds to almost every word I have ever written. For her constant reminders about Christian love, integrity, kindness, and courage, I am deeply indebted. If on any page I do not demonstrate that I speak the truth in love, even with those with whom I most strongly disagree, she is not at fault. Because of her invaluable help, she has earned another dedication.

You Are Our God; We Are Your People

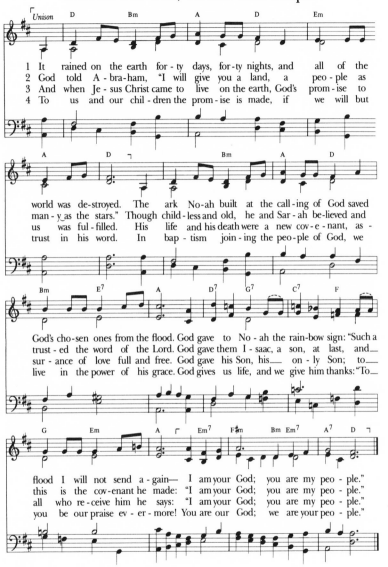

1 It rained on the earth for-ty days, for-ty nights, and all of the
2 God told A-bra-ham, "I will give you a land, a peo-ple as
3 And when Je-sus Christ came to live on the earth, God's prom-ise to
4 To us and our chil-dren the prom-ise is made, if we will but

world was de-stroyed. The ark No-ah built at the call-ing of God saved
man-y as the stars." Though child-less and old, he and Sar-ah be-lieved and
us was ful-filled. His life and his death were a new cov-e-nant, as-
trust in his word. In bap-tism join-ing the peo-ple of God, we

God's cho-sen ones from the flood. God gave to No-ah the rain-bow sign: "Such a
trust-ed the word of the Lord. God gave them I-saac, a son, at last, and
sur-ance of love full and free. God gave his Son, his on-ly Son; to
live in the power of his grace. God gives us life, and we give him thanks: "To

flood I will not send a-gain— I am your God; you are my peo-ple."
this is the cov-e-nant he made: "I am your God; you are my peo-ple."
all who re-ceive him he says: "I am your God; you are my peo-ple."
you be our praise ev-er-more! You are our God; we are your peo-ple."

Text and Tune: David A. Hoekema, 1978. © 1985, CRC Publications

Introduction

AT a June 1986 conference on "Christianity and the History of Science," Dr. Ronald L. Numbers from the University of Wisconsin posed a question which left all the participants in a quandary. Suppose, he said, that you had to make a choice between evolution and scientific creationism, on which side would you align yourself?

The twenty-four participants were all faculty members from the Christian College Coalition, which sponsored the conference and selected the participants on the basis of personal interest and the ability to make significant contributions to the ongoing debate between science and religion. The selection criteria for the conference did not include any kind of litmus test on the issues and assumed no balance of opinions on the controversy currently wracking American academia.

Not one of the participants was willing to make a commitment at first. Everyone had some kind of objection to the way the question was posed. After listening to a variety of hems, haws, yes-buts, and no-ifs, Numbers again pressed for a decision and gave his reasons for requiring a choice on one or the other side. The question, he asserted, is not simply an academic one, where numerous qualifiers may be attached and ingenious variations offered, but a legal one. The debate over creation vs. evolution has become a legal dispute, he reminded us, with judges and juries called to decide whether creationism may be legally taught in the public schools of the land. As "experts" on the subject, the conference participants would be called upon to take a stand, possibly in a court of law, but certainly in their classrooms. The judges on the bench, the lawyers presenting the case, and the students in the classrooms would not tolerate fence-straddling, yet-buts, and maybe-ifs. Given your reservations, on which side would you stand or fall?

Ron Numbers posed the choice for us because he was at the time confronted with that same dilemma. Because of his widely heralded expertise, lawyers for both sides in the Louisiana creation-evolution case wanted him as an expert witness when they filed their briefs with the United States Supreme Court. Neither side would tolerate his straddling the fence nor would they permit him to argue for both sides. Either you are for us, or you are against us, they said. You cannot argue credibly for opposing points of view, and you can only be neutral to the extent that you willingly promise to persuade no one, studiously avoid the issue, and refrain from coming to any personal conclusions. If you adopt such a stance, you will be of no use to us.

The conference participants were painted into a corner, much to their chagrin, and now had to step out on one side of the fence or the other. Those who would be willing to align with the creationists were asked to respond first. One hand went up. The other twenty-three chose to defend the evolutionists. I was surprised and lonesome, but unashamed. I had taken my stand and would repeat it if asked to make the same choice again. Given opportunity to explain my decision, I hastened to list some of my reservations about the political, legal, and pedagogical strategies that were being deployed by some persons and some groups in the creation-science movement. I also argued, however, that there was an overwhelming amount of Biblical and scientific evidence to support the conclusion that God had created the entire universe in a marvelous, mind-boggling fashion and that in a relatively recent historical period. I took my stand not only with Genesis 1–11, but also with numerous other Scriptures, including Job 37–41.

The reaction of my conference colleagues was pleasant and reassuring, yet disturbing. Privately more than a few confided to me that the biggest deterrence to their standing with me was their fear of professional rejection within the scientific community. The possibilities for research grants, publishing opportunities, and academic advancement would be minimized if they were labelled as creationists. Those admissions scared and disappointed me. What had happened to open-minded inquiry? to academic freedom? to Christian commitment? to Biblical distinctiveness?

Were all of them on their deathbed? Had secularism so gripped our Christian college faculties that almost no one was willing to risk the subtle persecutions dispensed by the majority?

That conference in Oregon made an indelible impression on my mind and serves to this day as the spur for the writing of this series of articles. Without that experience I probably would never have undertaken the arduous task of organizing, reading, analyzing, and writing the pages that are to follow.

Sorting through all the many dimensions of the debate between creationists and evolutionists is no simple task, for the problem is exceedingly complex. One cannot simply adopt a "scientific attitude," for "science" never has and never will exist in isolation. Only those who are radical secularists can pretend that "science" has the answers, but they ignore all the historical, philosophic, and religious trappings in which "science" has been wrapped since the beginning of our modern age.

As one committed unashamedly to a monistic worldview, with Christ as the one in whom all things cohere, I am propelled by a comprehensive faith to give an account of my beliefs. Those beliefs are not limited in some artificial, analytical fashion to a narrow set of concerns, but must be seen in relationship to such matters as science, knowledge, reason, unbelief, history, and behavior. They are set, furthermore, in a context of having to "test the spirits, to see whether they be of God," and of being "transformed by the daily renewing of the mind so that I may prove what is that good, pleasing, and perfect will of God."

What follows, then, is an imperfect, sometimes sketchy, probably obscure, effort to delineate the issues that make the current debate between creationists and evolutionists such a knotty problem. It has been dominating our intellectual efforts for more than a century and a half and probably will continue to plague the Western mind for decades to come. Until the final judgment, when all debate will mercifully be silenced, we will continue to hear arguments about if, when, and how God created the universe in which we live. Many will grow weary before then and hope that the battle will disappear if they just ignore it long enough.

Because I know that I will someday have to stand before that Great Judge who fashioned and sustains this marvelous creation, I want to take my stand while there is still time. Without knowing precisely how, when, or why He has created, controlled, and occasionally disturbed his fantastic design, I am confident that it belongs to God from beginning to end.

What follows, then is my "apology" for standing alone in Oregon during the summer of 1986 and many times since.

Truth by Counting?

It would have been easy to do my arithmetic and come to the conclusion that I was wrong. Twenty-three to one! The twenty-three almost all had advanced university degrees in biology, chemistry, astronomy, or geology. They had studied subjects in their labs, of which I had not even heard. Certainly the majority must have been right. Yet their own admissions, shared in private, gave me the courage to hold on to my convictions.

One of the ways we seek to bolster our own position is to see how many persons of like mind we can count on our side. In numbers there is strength. But in numbers evil and falsehood can also be multiplied. If Martin Luther had waited for a majority, we would never have had a Reformation. If Harriet Beecher Stowe had conformed to popular opinion, we would never have abolished slavery in the United States. If Van Raalte and Scholte had capitulated to the state church of the Netherlands, we would never had the Afscheiding.

But most people, myself included, prefer the safety of majority support. The National Academy of Sciences, for example, in a recent booklet mailed to every identifiable teacher of natural sciences in the United States, pleads for support of the evolutionary hypothesis by citing as evidence that "a great many religious leaders and scientists accept evolution on scientific grounds without relinquishing their belief in religious principles."[1]

Another example of such nose-counting was evident in the case in which the Supreme Court of Arkansas ruled that the Balanced Treatment Act was unconstitutional. Not willing to rely only on the "expert" testimony of natural scientists, the plaintiffs (i.e. the evolutionists) designed the strategy of recruiting as many ministers and religious leaders as possible to testify for evolution and against creation-science. In the balance of popular and judicial opinion it became evident that more big-name religious leaders were willing to speak for evolution than could be mustered against it.

We know, however, that might does not make right. The

majority may decide what is currently acceptable, but can never determine what is truth and what is falsehood. History is full of examples in which the vast majority were clearly in the wrong. Slavery is merely one obvious example. Even our ancestors who built the empire of the Dutch West Indies Company were active slave traders. The Nazi extermination of the Jews before and during World War II is another example. The radical separation of church and state is still another.

Although there is comfort in numbers, it should be apparent that we cannot reliably learn what is right simply by counting hands. Having a majority is no guarantee of right or wrong.

Conforming for Comfort?

But the question remains: why would the majority of science instructors at avowedly Christian colleges opt for theistic evolution rather than creation? Why would the majority of them openly affiliate with the American Scientific Affiliation (ASA), which espouses theistic evolution as its official stance?

The answer lies, I think, in *conformity*. It is easy to follow the crowd. It is professionally desirable to be published in refereed journals. It is laudable to be awarded research grants by the National Science Foundation. It is ego-fulfilling to have large organizations throwing academic bouquets in your direction. It feels better to be in the majority. I can understand and even appreciate that.

But conforming to this present world is a sin against which the Apostle Paul sternly warns us. "Do not conform any longer to the pattern of this world, but be transformed by the renewing of your mind"[2] is the first and foremost application of the gospel, as Paul has summarized it.

Yet conformity is so easy and so tempting. When all the power brokers and most of the dispensers of government grants are on the side of evolution, it is very difficult to stand in opposition. When the majority of textbooks from which our scientists have to study and teach are built on secular, evolutionary hypotheses it takes concerted efforts in critical reading not to be influenced by them.

During the past few decades evolutionary leaders have taken great pains to emphasize that science and religion are not at war. There must not be any conflict between church leaders and the scientific community, they say, because "religion and science are separate and mutually exclusive realms of human thought."[3] Such a pronouncement by the National Academy of Sciences is a wholly secular concept, unbecoming of anyone who wishes to be called Christian. It destroys the wholeness and cohesiveness of God's creation. It also is destroying the *uni*versities of our land and replacing them with *multi*-versities.

But such a secular notion has also crept into our own Christian colleges. Howard Van Til, for example, echoes an almost identical sentiment when he asserts,

> No authentic religious concept, ancient or modern, can be replaced by a scientific concept, ancient or modern. Substitution is impossible because science and religion deal with essentially different categories of questions.[4]

Conclusion

Are science and religion at war? Must the church be at odds with the scientific community? Must we choose *for* creation and *against* evolution? Are we confronted with an either/or or a both/and situation? Some answers next time, in Chapter 1.

CHAPTER ONE

Warfare Metaphor

HAVE you ever wondered about the irony implied in the term "theistic evolutionists"? How could a "theist," i.e., one who believes in God, accept the notion that evolution is true? Are not those two beliefs mutually exclusive? Why would twenty-three out of twenty-four "scientists" at a Christian college conference knowingly choose for evolution over against creation science?

The answer, I think, is that *they want peace. They dislike war.* They bleed too much and too often whenever war breaks out. Too many of their Christian friends in the profession could stand to lose jobs, income, influence, or prestige if war continues. On their respective campuses they cringe in fear everytime someone threatens to debate the creation-evolution controversy.

These men, and their rather infrequent female counterparts, are offspring of the peace era. For the most part, they did their undergraduate and graduate studies during the decades when university and college campuses were wracked with turbulence and wild-eyed protests. They have felt the sting of ideological warfare.

They have been affected, however, not only by the campus protests of the sixties and seventies. Their scholarly readings, conferences, and graduate studies have been saturated with stories of war. They can probably recite, backward and forwards, the details of "the Galileo affair" and the "Scopes Trial" of 1925.

Within this ideological camp of theistic evolutionists are large numbers who come out of the tradition of the Protestant Reformation and, more specifically, out of the Calvinistic, Reformed heritage. They are well versed in the concept that both the Scriptures and the creation, which we sometimes call "nature," are both

7

revelations of God. Since God gave us both His Word and His world, they would argue, the two cannot be at odds. As true Reformers, they love to recite Article II of the Confession of Faith.[5] In response to the question, By what means is God made known to us? they are quick to reply:

> We know Him by two means: First, by the creation, preservation, and governance of the universe, which is before our eyes as a most elegant book, and . . . second, He makes Himself more clearly and fully known to us by His holy and divine Word.

In that Protestant Reformation tradition, there cannot be conflict between God's Word and God's world. Warfare is a curse that comes from sin, and, although endured, is not to be desired. Warfare between science and faith is, then, not to be encouraged or even condoned, but to be condemned. Certainly there may be some in the camp of "Christian evolutionists" who love to fight and see war as just one more way to earn their scientific spurs.

For the most part, however, they plead for peace. We want peace, they say, even if we have to fight to get it. We want peace and will write to that end, even if we need to risk the charges of heresy in the process. Preferably, though, we would like the tranquility of an undisturbed classroom where we can quietly teach the next generation our peculiar road to peace. Grant us academic freedom so that we can proclaim our theistic and evolutionary views to our classes without risking our tenured positions. Leave us alone.

Does that kind of behavior appear ironic? Does that kind of talk ring discordant sounds in your ear? Is it a contradiction to fight for peace?

Most theistic evolutionists are not wimps. Like a cornered puppy, they will fight if sufficiently threatened. Their preferred battleground is the lecture hall, where they can easily challenge their outclassed opponents and win most every argument dealing with evolution. When pitted against a peer, however, most will beat a hasty retreat, hiding behind a plea for peace.

We Will Fight

One of the favorite strategies of theistic evolutionists is to pose for their audience an either/or question. It usually goes like this: Did God create the Grand Canyon, *or* was the Canyon carved out by a river?

If an atheist were asking the question, the answer would be simple. Since God does not exist, according to the atheist, the river would get the exclusive credit for creating the Grand Canyon, with all of its marvelous splendor. For the theistic evolutionist, however, the question is intended as a clever trap. If the responder should insist that God did it, the evolutionist would quickly reply that the river obviously was involved too, because rivers have tremendous power and have always been observed to carry silt and to carve new channels. Anyone with half an observant eye can testify to that. If, on the other hand, the audience said that the river created the Grand Canyon, the pious theist would quickly cajole them for having denied God, who always governs, directs, and upholds the universe in all its minute dimensions.

A clever ploy. Clever because the theistic evolutionist wants you to accept his argument that it was *both* God *and* nature, working together over millions and maybe even billions of years, that "created" the Grand Canyon. Once he has his reader or his listener accepting the idea that the answer should not be *either/or*, but *both* God *and* nature, he can then proceed to dig out his scales and his measuring rods to prove conclusively that it must have taken many millions of years to carve out a canyon that is over a mile deep.

Watch out for such trickery. Such argumentation is not as simple and innocent as it may seem, for there is a hidden and complex agenda involved in that strategy. What the evolutionist wants to accomplish is not simply an answer to questions about the formation of canyons. He wants to prove to you that science is not at war with Christianity. He wants you to stop being suspicious of scientists. He wants you to think that science and religion are really allies, long-lost lovers who went through a nasty divorce during the nineteenth century and who now want to be reunited in marital bliss.

Science and Christianity may have been at war in previous centuries and during most of the twentieth, but such fighting is unbecoming for Christians. What we want is to bring them back together in beautiful harmony, to have them work hand in hand, so that both God and science may be glorified. That is their hidden agenda, their grand strategy to win converts to their position. But watch out.

Is Science a P.O.W?

One of the recent books that decries the "warfare metaphor" is entitled *Science Held Hostage*.[6] On its cover is a picture of a presumed scientist bound to a chair with his hands tied behind him. We know he is a scientist because he is bald, bearded, and wearing a white coat. He is obviously a prisoner, but of whom?

One doesn't have to read far to recognize that the culprit, the terrorist who has bound and tied science, is religion. Theologians have invaded the domain of scientists. Ministers have hog-tied innocent, competent researchers. This kind of mischievous boundary-crossing must stop, for "the two are not enemies, but partners in the quest for understanding ourselves and the world."[7]

These same authors insist that "there exists no authoritative document" or "canonical source" which has the right to bind or restrict natural scientists.[8] Above all, terrorism and fighting must stop. Religion must be contained. Theologians may not meddle in areas that should be of no concern to them. Science must be free.

Was There a War?

One year after Charles Darwin published his infamous *Origin of Species*, an intense debate occurred between Thomas Henry Huxley (alias Darwin's Bulldog) and "Soapy Sam" Wilberforce at the 1860 meeting of the British Association for the Advancement of Science. Although there are many discrepancies in the various accounts of what really happened, an "official version" has been widely accepted and unchallenged, "not because we know its truth by copious documentation, but because so little data exists for a potential challenge."[9] That "official version," regrettably, was crafted by Darwin's supporters some twenty-five years after the event occurred. No doubt the debate was stimulating and significant because Huxley viewed it as another "battleground between science and organized religion—and he took great pride in the many notches on his own gun."[10]

Ever since the publication of Darwin's notorious book, science and religion have been at war, or at least so it seems. Every article, every book, and every speech was another shot fired. Platforms and lecture halls became battlefields. Pulpiteers became captains in the army, preparing Christian soldiers who were marching off to war. The protagonists paraded their ideological heroes through the public square for all to see and hear. Charles Darwin, Thomas Henry Huxley, Louis Agassiz, and Charles Lyell were obviously "generals" on the science side, while religion claimed Hodge and Wilberforce.

Charles Hodge, writing in 1874, insisted that it was "painfully notorious that there is an antagonism between scientific men as a class and religious men as a class. Of course the opposition is neither felt nor expressed by all on either side, . . . [but] there can be no doubt that it exists and that it is an evil."[11] Later he went on to assert, "Religion has to fight for its life against a large class of scientific men."[12]

The "warfare metaphor," as it has since been called, came to public acceptance after 1869, when Andrew Dickson White lectured to a large audience at the Cooper Union in New York City on "The Battle-Fields of Science." The address was carried the next day by the *New York Daily Tribune*, setting the tone for future historiography. Seven years later White published *The Warfare of Science*, which was followed by a series in the *Popular Science Monthly* on "New Chapters in the Warfare of Science." Finally, in 1896, he published the now classic, two-volume *History of the Warfare of Science with Theology in Christendom*. For the next century, White's magnum opus set the tone for what can accurately be called "the great debate." While the majority of his readers probably assumed that this was an objective, historical analysis, White himself made no claims to neutrality. "As the struggle deepened," he said, "I took the defensive and, in answer to various attacks from pulpits and religious newspapers, attempted to alloy the fears of the public. "Sweet Reasonableness" was fully tried, . . . [but] it soon became clear that to stand on the defensive only made matters worse."[13]

One year after White's *Warfare* was published, John William Draper followed suit with his *History of the Conflict Between Religion and Science*. In his preface he argued that "the history of Science is not a mere record of isolated discoveries; it is a narrative of two contending powers, the expensive force of the human intellect on one side, and the compression arising from traditionary faith and human interest on the other."[14] Draper made no secret of the fact that he was engaged in an open polemic against Christianity in general and Roman Catholicism in particular. Faith, he charged, was static, unchangeable, and anti-intellectual. In the

Catholic church, that traditional protector of the faith, we find that "the hands that are now raised in appeals to the Most Merciful are crimsoned. They have been steeped in blood."[15]

Science, on the other hand, "has never sought to ally herself to civil power. She has never attempted to throw odium or inflict social ruin on any human being. She has never subjected anyone to mental torment, physical torture, least of all death, for the purpose of upholding or promoting her ideas."[16] For Draper, as for White, science has been exalted to the place of God. Science was kind, intelligent, and progressive, always on the path of truth and right.

Thomas Henry Huxley had helped to put science in its position of prominence. As "the most eloquent spokesman that evolution has ever known," he developed an extreme anticlericalism which "led him to an uncompromising view of organized religion as the enemy of science."[17] Huxley could conceive of no allies among the official clergy of his era. The liberals, he said, "lacked the guts to renounce what fact and logic had falsified, as they struggled to marry the irreconcilable findings of science with their supernatural vision."[18] Conservatives like Wilberforce and Hodge, on the other hand, "were enemies pure and simple," [19] who at least had the good sense not to attempt impossible compromises.

Is the Metaphor Valid?

Although it is not difficult to find numerous examples of controversy in the history of Christianity and science, "recent scholarship has shown the warfare metaphor to be neither useful nor tenable in describing the relationship between science and religion."[20] According to Lindberg and Numbers, there is mounting evidence that Andrew Dickson White "read the past through battle-scarred glasses, that he and his imitators have distorted history to serve ideological ends of their own."[21]

Contrary to popular opinion, the Galileo affair "was not a matter of Christianity waging war on science. Everyone of the participants called himself a Christian and all acknowledged Biblical authority."[22] The same could be said for the controversies surrounding the writings of Copernicus, Keplar, and Newton. During those earlier centuries, and even now in the twentieth century, the most animated discussions have often occurred among Christians and have focused on the interpretation of specific passages in Scripture.

Once the inappropriateness of the warfare metaphor is admitted, we need to look further for an explanation of the conflict and controversy that is so obvious. To say that the war is not being fought between Christianity and science is not to say that there is no war. Certainly there has been open warfare between evolutionists and creationists, with both insisting that science is on their side.

Whoever the protagonists may be, it should be obvious to all that the conflict has not been, and should not be, between science and Christianity. The Christian church has always maintained a keen interest in the study of nature. Reformers such as Calvin, Knox, and Luther, for example, argued that there were "two books" through which God revealed Himself, first the "book of nature" and then the inscripturated Word. The study of stars, plants, animals, and inanimate creation has been a high obligation for the Christian because the material world is the very creation of God's hand and was designed to praise Him.

Conclusion

Theistic evolutionists are certainly correct when they decry the supposed war that has presumably been going on between science and Christianity. If science is correctly understood, it cannot be at war with the Christian faith. What has happened, however, is that theistic evolutionists, while persistently claiming to be defusing a war that never was, have actually fueled the fires of controversy to new levels of intensity. Books such as *The Fourth Day* and *Science Held Hostage* have fanned the flames, especially in Reformed, evangelical, and fundamentalist circles.

What the theistic evolutionists have done is to conjure up bad solutions to a perennial problem. They have tried to buy prestige and power at the expense of academic integrity. While claiming to be Reformed, they have been peddling concepts bought at the feet of Thomas Aquinas and Immanuel Kant. While pretending that they are opposed to the thinking of atheistic evolutionists, they insist on defining science in the same way as those they claim to be refuting. Those are strong charges, so let me explain.

One way to prevent or to stop a war is to put the enemies in separate worlds. If you want to stop the conflict in the Middle East, send the Jews to the South Pole and send the P.L.O. to the North Pole. If that is too drastic, build a wall so high that neither can scale it and make certain that all the characters are on the correct side.

In slightly more complex fashion, that is precisely the solution offered by the authors of *Science Held Hostage*. Science and theology, they claim, are mutually exclusive categories. Each has its own room. If we simply keep each one confined to that room, fighting cannot possibly occur. If you want answers to scientific questions, ask a scientist. If you want answers to theological questions, ask a theologian. If we all follow those rules, there will be no more fighting. The warfare metaphor can be put to bed and we may all sleep in peace.

Nice. But that "solution" is certainly not new and creates more problems than it pretends to resolve. Such a "solution" is analogous to employing a fox to guard your chicken coop. It invites secular humanists to solve Christian problems. That can never produce a happy conclusion.

Although theistic evolutionists would not like to admit it, they have also borrowed a strategy from Georg Friedrich Hegel. A decidedly non-Christian philosopher, Hegel articulated an approach to problem-solving which is most succinctly described by the terms *thesis, antithesis,* and *synthesis.* For every ideological idea, or thesis, there will develop its opposite or antithesis. After the advocates of these two positions engage in debate, a middle road of compromise is found, which is called a synthesis. This synthesis then becomes a new thesis, and the cycle is repeated. Through such dialogue, truth is advanced to a higher level.

Hegel's dialectic is appealing if you believe that truth is fluid and subject to revision. It allows for harmony or shalom after a brief debate. It will give the peace we all so desperately want.

The Bible, however, claims to be eternally true. It is unchanging truth for a changing world. God's Word is as true today as it was for Abraham, David, and Paul. It doesn't adapt to the changing beliefs of differing generations. No, the generations have to adjust their thinking to it.

In spite of those eternal truth claims for the Christian gospel, theistic evolutionists have borrowed the Hegelian system. Setting up creation science as the thesis, they have posited naturalistic evolution as the antithesis. Then, in ingenious fashion, they have combined the two to form their position of theistic evolution. A perfect synthesis, they claim. We will war no more, if you all accept our solution.

CHAPTER TWO

The Real War

A long time ago, I think it was in 1948 and 1949, I was a student at a little Christian school in Rock Valley, Iowa. The school only had four classrooms, with two grades in each. My principal-teacher was an unusual man named Mr. J.C. Lobbes. I'll never forget him or what he taught us. He made us read sections of Charles Darwin's *The Origin of Species*. I'll also never forget the look on my father's face when he once saw me with that book in my hands. Horrors!

But my dad really did not have to fear. Old J.C. was simply teaching us *about* evolution. He didn't want us to believe it. In fact, he worked diligently, day in and day out, to help us critique and analyze that devilish theory in such a way that we would never believe it. What he wanted and what he was profoundly successful at, was for all of us to believe in the creation account from Scripture. He knew, however, that we would be bombarded with evolutionary ideas outside of school, on the streets, in newspapers, in magazines, on the radio, and even at national parks and museums. Evolution was being propagated everywhere. So he skillfully engaged us in a dangerous business in a safe place. There was no neutrality in his classroom. We were simply and surely being prepared for ideological warfare that was certain to come.

At almost the same time, in Grand Rapids, Michigan, Dr. John De Vries was putting together his manuscript for *Beyond the Atom*. In the Preface he wrote, "This book is addressed primarily to orthodox Christians in an attempt to strengthen their faith." As a highly respected chemistry professor at Calvin College, he set out to study and explain the relationship of the inorganic sciences to our faith. In an attitude closely paralleling that of my seventh and eighth grade teacher, De Vries remarked,

> The study of the sciences challenges the youth of today. They will go where they can obtain such knowledge. Where shall we send them? To schools where the instructors deny and ridicule God, or, at best, just ignore Him? Do not misunderstand me. We should study their teachings thoroughly in order that we may meet them victoriously. We should study the materialistic philosophies of the past in great detail. With that as a background we should attack those of the present before they lead too many men farther astray.

Some twenty-odd years after those two events, our oldest son was in a departmentalized public junior high school. He had a certain geography teacher who almost never taught geography. Somehow he had come to the conclusion that his major mission in life was to persuade everyone of the truth of evolution. Greg came home each day with accounts of new "scientific stuff" he had encountered. Our evening conversations, quite naturally, turned to that subject with increasing regularity. Finally, in frustration, we arranged a conference with the teacher. No success and no satisfaction. Then off to the principal, who portrayed himself as a blend between the great pacifist and the protector of his professional staff. Finally, in desperation, we realized that Greg could not be given a deferment any longer. He would have to fight his own war, with our assistance.

Each night after dinner, I would quiz him on the day's lesson in evolution. I would then analyze the information with him and suggest some questions which he could pose to his instructor the next day. Confronted each class period by a series of tough questions, the teacher soon found it convenient to get back into his geography text. Another battle won.

Its Spiritual Character

In our last article we described the war that supposedly had gone on between "science" and Christianity during the nineteenth and into the twentieth centuries. We concluded, quite correctly, we think, that no such war could possibly exist because science, rightly understood as knowledge, is itself a gift from God and His ultimate possession. What Andrew White and William Draper were trying to describe was both badly misinterpreted and grossly mislabeled.

But there is and has been warfare. It is not just a metaphor, but a real war. It has been going on ever since the Garden of Eden, where God said to Satan,

> I will put enmity
> between you and the woman,
> and between your offspring and hers;
> he will crush your head,
> and you will strike his heel (Gen. 3:15).

That warfare is also described for us in powerful, dramatic, visionary imagery in Revelation 12. The apostle John there describes for us the drama he saw unfolding before his eyes. He tells us,

> And there was war in heaven. Michael and his angels fought against the dragon, and the dragon and his angels fought back. But he was not strong enough, and they lost their place in heaven. The great dragon was hurled down—that ancient serpent called the devil or Satan, who leads the whole world astray (vs. 7–9a).

Those familiar with that chapter will remember that this visionary drama has three main characters: the woman, the male child, and the dragon. The male child is obviously Christ, who was already foretold in Gen. 3:15. The dragon is clearly identified as Satan. The woman, on the other hand, is most difficult to identify precisely. At one level, the portrayal is certainly that of the mother Mary, but, on another level, she is also Eve. Most importantly, the woman refers to the church of both the Old and the New dispensations. The church, here and elsewhere throughout Scripture, is the Bride of Christ who is locked in a life and death struggle against the militaristic power of Satan.

Believers in Christ who make up that church are not deferred from the battle nor immune to the warfare. The apostle Paul makes that abundantly clear in his letter to the Ephesians. In his concluding remarks, he tells them and also us:

> Put on the full armor of God so that you can take your stand against the devil's schemes. For our struggle is not against

flesh and blood, but against the rulers, against the authorities, against the powers of this dark world and against the
spiritual forces of evil (Eph. 6:11–12).

In some Christian traditions, this warfare has been referred to as
"spiritual conflict," which it most certainly is. Others, however,
refer to it as "the great antithesis." In simple diagram form, it looks
like this:

THE ANTITHESIS

GOD	vs.	SATAN
TRUTH	vs.	FALSEHOOD
WISDOM	vs.	FOOLISHNESS
GOOD	vs.	EVIL
LIGHT	vs.	DARKNESS
LIFE	vs.	DEATH
NOAHIC FLOOD	vs.	ICE AGE THEORY
CREATION	vs.	EVOLUTION
CHRISTIANITY	vs.	SECULARISM

It is quite probable that some theorists would prefer to redraw the
above formulation. Some may object, for example, to the placing
of the Noahic flood and ice age theory as antitheticals. Others may
complain that creation and evolution should not be opposites, but
should be melded into some sort of creationomic or theistic evolution. Regardless of such reactions, everyone has some kind of
model that they would advance. Every ideological stance has an
antithetical relationship to its opposite. The only question is how
we draw the model and what we include.

Missing the Mark

In all the stories told by White and Draper, there was obviously a
misunderstanding of the war's real character. But theirs is not the
only instance where the military historians had failed to identify
correctly the real protagonists. History is full of conflicts, where
either one or both sides mislabeled the enemies and fought wars that
missed the mark.

One of the most enduring conflicts, and one that has nagged for
Western attention for over one hundred and fifty years now, is that

going on between creationists and evolutionists. In some respects it has been a mean, nasty, despicable kind of engagement. But wars are never pretty. We might all wish that we would never see another one. When one picks up a respected newspaper and views a cartoon like the one printed below, one is inclined to cancel the subscription and boycott all its advertisers.

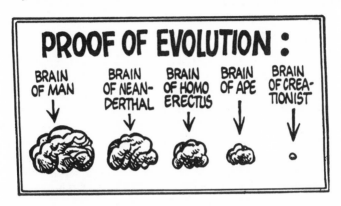

But then one reads on and realizes the stupidity of the opposition, and one can only laugh in derision. The following news item was printed under the headline, "Smile, while you have it."

> **Smile, while you have it**
> ANN ARBOR—Human teeth are becoming smaller because of modern cooking practices, according to a University of Michigan researcher.
>
> Teeth have shrunk about 50 percent in the past 100,000 years, and the process is continuing, said C. Loring Brace, a U-M professor of anthropology.
>
> Tooth size is decreasing at a rate of about 1 percent every 1,000 years, Brace said. He said that as softer foods have become available over the years, humans have had less need of big, strong teeth to survive.

Appearing in the same paper at a later date, it was apparent that the intent of the editorial staff was to publish some more propaganda in support of their pet prejudice. The quality of the ammunition, however, is so pathetic that the only legitimate response would be uproarious laughter. By what kind of observable, verifiable, and repeatable laboratory procedure could this "scientist" have acquired evidence that "tooth size is decreasing at a rate of about 1 percent every one thousand years"? How many teeth did he examine? Which variables was he able to control? Who did his research one thousand years ago? Two thousand years ago? One hundred thousand years ago?

The Focal Point

If one loses the perspective of Scripture, it is almost certain that the battle between creationists and evolutionists will lose its proper focus. It would be easy to become so engrossed in tracking the shrapnel of detail and wildly aimed missiles that one could take his eyes off of God's promises and God Himself. It could then become a futile effort, an unwinnable war, a cause for depression, and a reason for surrender. But such dejection should not occur.

The war is ultimately not our war, but God's war. He is the original defender, and Satan the original assailant. The good news, however, is that God has already won. Victory was assured almost two thousand years ago on a hillside outside of Jerusalem, and we "are more than conquerors through him who loved us" (Rom. 8:37).

Yet the war drags on. It is not in Satan's character to admit defeat, so he still goes raging throughout the world like a roaring lion seeking whom he may devour. He still lies with reckless abandon, hoping to entice some gullible soul to swallow his pretentious claims to the throne of God.

Seen in that light, we can recognize that this is no mere scientific dispute, no mere ideological difference, but a *spiritual* warfare between the King of the Universe and an angelic pretender. As such, it is serious business. At stake is the allegiance of every believer, for it is a war that involves all of us. It is a spiritual warfare that goes on within the hearts and minds of every individual for commitment to Christ or commitment to the anti-Christ.

By the instigation of the devil and by their own free will, Adam and Eve listened to the tempting distortions of Satan and rejected God's authoritative pronouncements. In the language of Romans, they "exchanged the truth of God for a lie, and worshipped and served created things rather than the Creator" (1:25). As descendants of Adam, we, too, fight those same battles within ourselves. There are the traditions and beliefs that we have been taught from childhood on. There are the rights and wrongs that we learned in Sunday school, in church, and at our parents' sides. Then suddenly there come new ideas, new beliefs, and new theories, and new standards for right and wrong. Naturally there is conflict. Whom and what do we believe? What is true? What is false?

Onward Christian Soldiers

There is an old familiar hymn, written some six years after *The Origin of Species* was published, which depicts us as soldiers, "marching as to war." There have been repeated attempts to discredit the song on the grounds that it is too militaristic. In most orthodox traditions the song has endured, as have others with similar themes. The reason for retention is not merely sentiment, but a keen awareness that we who comprise the church are God's agents on earth; we are His vice-regents and are called to advance His kingdom here below.

We can pretend to ignore the battle still being waged by Satan against the church of God, but such a stance denies the repeated teaching of Scripture and does our children a terrible disservice. Satan constantly tries to entice us to his side and often succeeds without our realizing it. Christ made that plain when he scolded the tempestuous Peter with that stinging rebuke, "Get behind me, Satan." C.S. Lewis demonstrates that same clever conniving of Satan by dozens of illustrations in his *Screwtape Letters*.

In order to understand this warfare correctly, we need to see it also as a conflict between truth and falsehood. Ever since the onslaughts of pragmatic philosophy, we have not been as cognizant of these terms as our ancestors were. Today we become preoccupied with whether a concept "works" and not whether it is true. The message of Scripture, though, is that we should "get wisdom" and "hold fast to truth." In order to do that, we need to know what those terms mean. The following definitions are based on careful studies of Biblical meaning:

WISDOM: Knowing the Truth and Living in Accord with it

| The Word | Truth | Christ |

Truth: 1. The Word of God (Ps. 119:160)
      2. Jesus Christ, The Word Incarnate
         I am the way, the Truth, the Life (John 14:6)
      3. All propositions that are in Harmony with the Word
         of God

Falsehood: A Distortion or Perversion of the Truth
              Satan "is a liar, and the father of lies." Jn.8:44

Notice particularly the definition of falsehood. It is not the *opposite* of truth, nor the *absence* of truth, but a *distortion* or *perversion* of it. That is also the definition of a lie. All that Satan needs to do is twist the truth of Scripture a few degrees. That is what he did with Eve in the Garden. That is what he did to Peter, who, when he gullibly swallowed the distortion, earned Christ's stinging rebuke.

Every falsehood has some truth in it. That is precisely what makes it so tempting and so subtle. But that is also why discernment between truth and falsehood is sometimes so difficult. Knowing when we have been lied to is not always easy to determine.

If we fail to teach our children the difference between truth and falsehood, we will be guilty of sticking our heads in the sand like the proverbial ostrich. And if we think that "science" is as neutral as dialing a telephone, we will have closed our eyes to reality. The student in school, the man on the street, and the visitor to a museum are always confronted with statements which are either true or false. Let me illustrate.

The following set of questions might be typical of statements we all encounter and to which we either have to give assent or express disagreement. In the format of a quiz, take a minute to mark them either true or false.

      _____ 1. The earth was created at least 14.5 billion years ago.

      _____ 2. The Bible is not a textbook of science.

      _____ 3. There is no scientific evidence for a worldwide flood.

      _____ 4. Scripture and science deal with mutually exclusive sets of questions.

_____ 5. The first eleven chapters of Genesis cannot be interpreted literally.

Whether we answer the above questions as true or as false will be profoundly important for any subsequent discussion. Ideas are not simply true or false; they also have consequences.

Conclusion

When we try to determine whether a statement is true or false, we are not merely engaging in an academic exercise. We are not simply trying to get a high score on a quiz or test. In its most profound sense, we are trying to "test the spirits, to see whether they are from God, because many false prophets have gone out into the world" (I John 4:1).

What we have in the evolutionary movement is the attempt by Satan and his allies to erode the truth of God's Word. His authorship is called into question. His "scientific" expertise is denied. God and His book cannot be trusted for historical accuracy. The Genesis account is simply, especially in its first eleven chapters, a myth used to convey some theological meaning. In its most crass form, the debaters confront us with the question—whom are you going to believe: God or Darwin?

The war is real, but is not between science and Christianity. It is between God and Satan. Like the Israelites of Joshua's day, we simply have to decide on which side we choose to serve.

CHAPTER THREE

What is Science?

WE were sitting around the lunchroom table, five of us in all. We had been ruminating on a discussion held two days earlier in our monthly faculty forum. The topic had been the creation-evolution debate, hardly a dead issue on most campuses. In response to some impassioned remarks about "scientists," I pointedly asked a colleague who had been most vociferous, "How many scientists are at this table right now?" He looked rather pensively for a few seconds and then said, "One."

"Who is it?" I asked, with a twinkle in my eye.

His reply surprised me only a little. I knew he didn't think of me as a scientist, for I specialized in training future teachers. I knew that he wasn't thinking of himself, for he prided himself on being an artist. And I did not expect him to label the two psychology professors, even though they were openly hoping that he would point the finger at them and had forgotten how to count.

He finally pointed the finger at a professor of obstetrical nursing, who was more than a little surprised. "Why me?" she asked.

"You are a scientist because you are at least partially involved in the field of medicine."

By now all five minds were in high gear. Why did she, a nurse, deserve that distinction?

Why isn't psychology a science? Why don't you deserve to be called a scientist if you deliberately and frequently employ the scientific method?

It is no secret that we live in what is often called "the Age of Science." During the 1970s, the Council for Financial Aid to Education ran an ad campaign under the heading, "80% of the

scientists who have ever lived are alive today." That kind of propaganda brought millions of dollars into their coffers, even though
most people never questioned the statement or probed its
ambiguous meanings. "Throw money in the direction of science"
would have been a more candid and honest statement.

The problem is not with science, as we have pointed out earlier in
"The Warfare Metaphor." The problem is that almost no one
bothers to define science. We keep using a term that very few, including those who proudly call themselves "scientists," begin, or
even try, to understand. The situation is almost as ridiculous as it
would be if some devious teacher went to a preschool and chanted
repeatedly to three-year-olds, "You are all philanthropists" until
they all memorized the sounds and then repeated the term in every
conceivable encounter. We would all look askance and wonder
who had put such meaningless terminology into their heads.

When we use the word "science" without the faintest notion of its
meaning, we are no different than those three-year-olds. Yet the
words "science" and "scientific" have become tremendously significant words in our culture. The intellectual climate is such that the
mere use of such charismatic words almost magically makes one
deserving of high praise for coming into possession of marvelous
new discoveries. To be unscientific, by contrast, is to be uninformed, at best, or stupid and senseless, at worst. To charge a
person with being unscientific is to heap coals of condemnation on
his head.

For many people, Science must always be capitalized. Science,
if not possessing divine qualities, is certainly a powerful, personal
force that is capable of curing cancer, discovering new chemical
elements, dating fossils, and sending space shuttles into orbit.
Science can accomplish almost anything. For such people, science
is to be worshipped, not defined.

For the Christian, however, such an attitude is simply un-
acceptable. The holy and jealous God of the Scriptures would never
brook such presumptuous deification or even the lesser evil of
personification. God did not create science in the image of Himself
or even make it a little lower than the angels. No, "science" falls
into some other category. For Christians at least, science must be
defined, not worshipped.

A perusal of any standard dictionary will indicate that the root
meaning of "science" is *knowledge*. In ancient Latin we find the

words scientia, sciens, and scire, which were translated respectively as "knowledge," "knowing," and "to know." This classical meaning has been transmitted down through the ages into western culture and was utilized by the English, French, and Germans with little variation in meaning until the middle of the nineteenth century.

Knowledge, or science, was something to be acquired or something that one could hold in possession, but it never took on personal or divine qualities. Everyone would have looked askance, for example, if anyone had labelled a person who had acquired some knowledge as being a "knowledgist." Yet that is essentially what Reverend William Whewell, a Cambridge philosopher of science, attempted in 1834. He coined the word "scientist," but provoked little more than incredulous stares. In 1840 he reasserted the usefulness of his newly coined term, but it enjoyed very little acceptance until almost 1900. Prior to that time there had always been a sharp distinction between knowledge and the knower. Whewell obliterated that distinction. He personified that which was not a person.

In 1874 Charles Hodge could still assert that "science, according to its etymology, is simply knowledge."[23] Hodge was taking note of meaning-shifts which had occurred particularly in England and the United States. The same, however, had not occurred in the German language, which retained the original, broader meaning of knowledge. Hodge went on to observe that in the German, the word *wissenschaft* is used of all kinds of knowledge. In that historic German sense, all five of the professors at our table should be called scientists, including the artist and the educator.

A second definition of science is closely harmonized with the first. Science is not merely knowledge, but also the preserved collections of knowledge which have been categorized and classified as academic disciplines. Historically we have done this classifying and grouping according to the object or focal point of our study. In the twentieth century, however, there have been concerted efforts to classify knowledge according to the "methodology" of study, an approach which, says David Lindberg, "is fraught with all kinds of danger." To claim that there is one category of knowledge which has exclusive right to the scientific or inductive approach, another which exclusively uses the rational or deductive approach, and still another which relies on faith is to admit a woeful ignorance of epistemology and to fabricate categories which are both false and artificial.

When "science" is understood as either knowledge or a systematic arrangement of knowledge into categories, there is no reason to be afraid of science, per se. But there is no reason to worship it either. For all of us, whether we be farmers or professors, bankers or housewives, biologists or musicians, to claim that we have a right to the scientific label and to be called scientists is then very legitimate. Each of us may have some knowledge that the others do not possess, but all of us are woefully ignorant in areas where others shine. Not one of us can claim sole possession of science or superiority over the others, except in our narrow field of concentration. When such occurs, the luster and gloss of "science" will be gone, but that forebodes no tragic consequence for the intellectual marketplace.

Because of common usage, we can employ a third definition of "science," namely, a method of study by which knowledge is acquired. When we think of science as a method of study, we are simply thinking of one of the ways by which all students and researchers work. It is frequently dubbed the "inductive approach," whereby we proceed from specific cases to general conclusions. The most common label for this procedure is "the scientific method." Everyone at our table that day rightly insisted and promptly illustrated that he or she used that method frequently.

When using the "scientific method," the researcher proceeds through the following generally stated steps:

a. Formulation of an hypothesis or theory to be proven;
b. Selection of events or phenomena to be examined;
c. Observation and categorization of the selections;
d. Generalization from those observations to all other similar events and phenomena; and
e. Drawing conclusions and formulating laws on the basis of these observations.

Some people who make their living by doing research try to pretend that the scientific method is a highly complicated, narrow, technical type of activity. In one sense that is true, particularly if one is doing research on dangerous, explosive chemicals or on nuclear fission. In another sense, though, the method is as uncomplicated and common as counting yes and no answers to a simple question. Both parties use the scientific method in essentially the same way. The only difference is that some scientists do their research with more potentially dangerous elements.

When "science" is understood in its classic, dictionary definitions, there is no reason to fear it and no reason to worship it. Science cannot be at war against Christianity and cannot do a thing. It cannot send space capsules to the moon. It cannot date fossils. It cannot predict the weather. It cannot create new surgical techniques. It cannot prove the age of the earth. Science, above all, cannot prove any evolutionary theory to be true. Only human beings can attempt such efforts, but they can utilize the knowledge they have acquired to enhance those efforts. As humans, they stand in allegiance either to the God of the universe or to the great Satanic pretender to that throne. When they are in Satan's employ and then use all the science that is available to them, we better be on guard lest we, too, come under his influence.

Turf Wars

In many of our large cities we have a great deal of difficulty with street gangs. Usually composed of insecure adolescents or post-adolescents, gangs make very concerted and often dangerous efforts to protect their turf. A given neighborhood or area "belongs" to a particular gang and must be guarded against all intruders. Every gang has its unique symbols, signs, and permits for passage. If a rival gang so much as wears the wrong-colored shoelaces or dares to walk on the wrong side of an alley, its members run the risk of a gang war.

In many ways, the boundary disputes among scientists represent that same deep-seated insecurity and senseless need to protect their turf. Numerous theistic evolutionists bristle with emotion whenever someone from outside their close-knit group dares to challenge their "scientific" assertions. If that challenger should be from the creationist camp, the epithets fly fast and furious. "You are not a scientist" is the usual charge, followed by such characterizations as "dishonest," "biased," and "prejudiced." In addition to the blatantly unchristian character of such attacks, they really display a deep-seated insecurity that calls into question the authenticity of their belief patterns.

At the same time that we detect these patterns of insecurity, there are also indicators of a false triumphalism. Just as each street gang claims to be in possession of great power, so the members of the natural sciences claim to be the Queen of the Sciences. Whereas theologians and philosophers had claimed that lofty seat during the late medieval era, now it is the biologists, chemists, astronomers, and geologists who pretend to have triumphed. As queens of academia, they can rewrite history, redefine the nature of man, and reinterpret the Scriptures. Traditional religious doctrines must be rejected because new, scientific theories have been advanced. According to them, the first eleven chapters of Genesis may no longer be interpreted literally because "science" has proven them to be mythological word pictures and prescientific fables.

If natural scientists would limit themselves to their own turf, as they so deceptively claim to be doing, there would certainly be less controversy, especially among Christians. But when they overstep their boundaries, turf wars erupt with expected and sometimes tragic consequences.

The Assumptions Behind Their Claims

In trying to exclude all competitors or in trying to force all other disciplines into the mold of the natural sciences, certain presuppositions or assumptions are almost always made. These are not unique to the natural scientist, but they are essential to the mode of operation used by the advocates of evolution.

Although there are numerous unproven assumptions on which evolutionary theory rests, there is one that deserves special attention. It is the assumption that all of physical reality is and has always been orderly and consistent. Those who hold to it most tenaciously, however, prefer not to discuss it or even acknowledge its existence, for it represents the Achilles heel of scientism. Its most common name is *uniformitarianism,* representing a deep-seated belief in the uniformity of the laws of nature across time and space.

The concept of natural laws and their uniform application derives from the Age of Enlightenment and the mechanistic worldviews of the seventeenth and eighteenth centuries. Holding yet to a belief in God, the mechanists and their deist counterparts constructed a clockwork image with a universe elaborately designed and tuned so that it ran like a precision clock. In the process of constructing a wholly continuous, atomistic world of natural laws immutably embedded in nature, they not only changed our conception of nature, but also our conception of nature's God. For the deists and for those who continue in their train, God became a cosmic legislator, a grand governor, a deific designer, and a sustainer of the clockwork image. No longer was He the righteous and angry Creator Who, in His righteous fury, upset the world with a cataclysmic flood. No longer was He Emmanuel, God with us, Who intervened in nature for the sake of His people. No longer was He "our God" or "our Father," Who disciplined His people because He loved them. On the contrary, He was merely the One who designed natural laws and set them in motion.

When Sir Charles Lyell published his *Principles of Geology* in 1830, the relevance of God to scientific activity had eroded even further. Since God was merely the clockmaker and since the clock was the object of study, He could be conveniently ignored. The value of all scientific study, Lyell concluded, "must depend entirely on the degree of confidence which we feel in regard to the permanence of the laws of nature."[24] Some fifteen years later Louis Agassiz applied the very same principle to his study of glaciers and then deduced, albeit quite illogically, that most of the northern hemisphere had for some time been covered with ice. A scant fifteen years further down the road Charles Darwin utilized the same uniformitarian argument to develop *The Origin of Species*. He, like all uniformitarian scientists, worked "with observable, gradual, small-scale changes and extrapolated their effects through immense time to encompass the grand phenomena of history."[25]

There is something highly fascinating and believable about such a clockwork image, such time-honored constancy and uniformity. A universe that presumably works in exactly the same way all the time is a real source of comfort and confidence, especially when God is so far removed in His role as designer and observer. For those who practice scientism, the uniformity of the laws of nature become their cardinal principle of faith, quite unlike that of the Christian who starts with "And God said."

The person who puts his faith in science and scientific progress is displaying "faith in the intrinsic goodness of human nature and in the omnipotence of science. It is a defiant and blasphemous faith, not unlike that held by the men who set out to build 'a city and a tower, whose top may reach unto heaven' and who believed that 'nothing will be restrained from them, which they have imagined to do.'"[26]

Conclusion

In one sense, it is depressing to come to the realization that "science" is no more powerful than a bag of sticks and stones. In a culture where scientism (the worship of science) runs rampant, it is disconcerting to realize that one of our cultural idols has been reduced to the level of common knowledge. The hopes and dreams of a grand design are gone. Our idol has proven to be nothing more than a hollow, speechless, powerless idol. Of course that will make some people despondent.

But there is an alternative view. Knowledge and science are still legitimate. The words of Proverbs still stand. "Hold on to instruction, do not let it go; guard it well, for it is your life" (4:13). Pursue knowledge, ask God for insight and understanding, but in all your efforts, remember, "The fear of the Lord is the beginning of wisdom" (1:7).

Knowledge is a gift from God. Because it is a gift, we must not worship it. Instead, we must give praise and thanks to the Giver, Who alone is the source of all knowledge, the only One Who has all knowledge in His possession. When we worship the gift and ascribe power to it, we are guilty of scientism. When we see knowledge as a gift from God, we can direct all our worship to Him alone.

CHAPTER FOUR

The Power of Persuasion

ONE of my professors at the University of Iowa was nearing retirement, but had been lured to the corn state to close out his teaching career. During his long tenure at the University of Chicago he had earned the appellation of "father of American religious historians." Sidney Mead had written a number of books, since used as texts at numerous graduate schools. Many university students came to Iowa primarily to study under him and hear his insightful lectures, but I just happened to be there.

Professor Mead was a brilliant scholar, a fatherly gentleman, a pleasant personality, and a supportive member of my doctoral research committee. But he was also a Unitarian and proud of it. He knew the Scriptures well, but quietly rejected the central message of Christ's divinity, even though he refused ever to let that become an issue in his classes. He taught for the School of Religion, but insisted that his personal religion was irrelevant to his understanding and interpretation of American religious history.

I knew instinctively that I had to be on guard. Having heard numerous sermons on the necessity of spiritual warfare, on rightly dividing the Word of truth, and on putting on the whole armor of God, I was historically conditioned to challenge any statement that did not harmonize with Scripture. Trained as a debater throughout my high school years and warned by numerous loved ones to hold onto the faith of our fathers, I was ready to challenge any Prof, no matter how prestigious. But the Bible said nothing about American religious history or whether it was true that the United States Constitution was a noble experiment in self-government. Were most of the Founding Fathers really Deists, as Mead insisted? Was the

Supreme Court correct in its interpretation of the Constitution, when they repeatedly insisted that there had to be a separation of church and state?

In spite of all my efforts to the contrary, I was duped by Sidney Mead and never realized it until some eight years later. In his quiet, effective, inimical way he had convinced me of his perspective on American history which later turned out to be seriously distorted. Through the providence of God, that vision became largely corrected, leaving me no option but to recant many of the ideas I had conveyed to my students over those intervening years![27]

Was our professor consciously, deliberately trying to deceive us? Was he, either overtly or covertly, attempting to frame an historical picture that would effectively eliminate the power of Christianity from American public life? Was he subtly advocating his own Unitarian beliefs and that of his intellectual forefathers?

As far as we could determine, the famous professor was an honest and open person. His students could disagree with him publicly and challenge his claims, without him ever being offended or flustered by their queries. With amazing serenity and massive doses of facts for rebuttal, he quickly set the challenger straight and proceeded with his lecture. Our only recourse was to acquiesce and believe. His was the power to persuade even the most wary.

How Do We Persuade?

Some years ago Bernard Bailyn produced a powerful book entitled *Education in the Forming of American Society.* The foci of his stinging criticisms were the American educational historians who had flooded the market with purportedly objective historical texts, books which were really apologies for secular public schools. More recently Paul Vitz authored his *Censorship: Evidence of Bias in our Children's Textbooks,* which graphically depicted for us how publishers had effectively eliminated all religious influences from the elementary and secondary textbooks dealing with the history of the United States. Most of what they had said about our past was worthy of belief, but what they had *not* said was far more important. The same was true for Sidney Mead. What he taught us was factual and beyond rebuttal. But what he did *not* teach us was of even greater import.

One does not have to work with historians very long before one realizes that there is no such thing as genuine neutrality. History writers are, like the rest of the human race, valuing, judging, and selecting individuals. They all have their value systems and priority scales, using them either consciously or subconsciously to focus on, cull out, and hold up for public examination that which they consider to be important. In their efforts to inculcate a world and life perspective, they fill their lectures and writings with those details and interpretations that will buttress their primary themes. In every research effort and in every publication, the material that is unknown, ignored, glossed over, or rejected far exceeds that which is extracted for dissemination. That exclusion makes a profound difference in the picture that is portrayed.

Wolterstorff put it this way, "No one of us can teach everything, nor can all of us together. Some things must be stressed and brought to the fore; others must be allowed to recede into the penumbra . . . . Few of a man's decisions are of more consequence than his decisions as to what he shall teach to his fellows and what he shall not."[28]

There is a myth rampant in our culture that defines education as merely information gathering and skill acquisition. Some identify it as the myth of neutrality. Predicated on the Lockean and Skinnerian notion that the mind is a blank slate at birth, the myth establishes the idea that a teacher's job is merely to impart or disseminate information, while the student's task is absorption. Countless students fit the mold, ready to fill their notebooks and their minds with whatever the teacher proclaims. Their least ambition is to think or question or challenge the instructor. Tell me what I need to know for the next test is their most fervent wish, a desire with which too many pedagogues are happy to comply.

One of the contemporary scholars who wrestles with this myth of neutrality and then gets all tangled in its web is Howard Van Til. Author of *The Fourth Day,* he argues there,

> But when a scientist is performing the technical tasks of investigating only the internal affairs of the material world, is it then possible to operate in a religiously neutral manner? Or are even technical operations such as observation, measurement, data analysis, and theoretical modeling affected by the scientist's religious faith? I am convinced that at this time in the history of science, they need not and ought not be affected . . . Natural science performed in the manner that we have described can be as religiously neutral as dialing a telephone.[29]

Van Til then goes on to ask, "but is natural science actually carried out in that manner?" To which he answers, "My personal judgment, based on more than twenty years of experience, is that the vast majority of professional scientific work is performed and reported in a manner that honors the categorical boundaries and stays within the legitimate domain of natural science . . . Textbooks do a reasonably good job of maintaining religious neutrality."[30]

For those familiar with the scene, it is ironic to note that *The Fourth Day* is one of the most controversial books published by the evangelical Christian community during the 1980s.[31] Part of the reason for the controversy is that Van Til, who claims neutrality for himself and most other natural scientists, spares no passion when he denounces those who disagree with him. In one of his frequent diatribes against "scientific creationism," he charges, "I am fully convinced that 'scientific creationism' is a travesty of natural science and a sad parody of Biblical theology."[32]

In one of my personal confrontations with that same author, he passionately pleaded with me never to tell my students that there was a Noahic flood. "There simply is no scientific evidence for one," he insisted.

Such hardly sounds like objective, neutral science. More like passionate persuasion, although I was not moved to reject the Genesis account.

Lest the reader get the wrong impression, Van Til is no different than you or I or your favorite teacher. He, like all mankind, holds to certain basic, core beliefs and will do everything in his power to convince us that those beliefs are valid and ought to be accepted by everyone. When one of his fundamental assertions is challenged, he, too, will bristle in defense and resort to whatever tactic will protect his ideological stance. If he is any different, it probably lies in his persuasive powers and in the core beliefs to which he holds.

Is Neutrality Possible?

Having said all that about persuasion, we still need to ask the question whether genuine neutrality is possible. Does the myth of neutrality contain any element of truth? Are teachers really presenting neutral facts, or are they always trying to persuade?

The answer to the above question hinges on the meaning of

neutrality. Neutrality is a military term and depicts a state of affairs when fighting has stopped or been prevented. For example, Switzerland has long prided itself on being able to stay out of the wars that ravaged Europe. The Swiss love to stay out of war. They are, therefore, neutral.

The same can be said for many classroom teachers. They do not want to fight. They prefer to lecture, illustrate their concepts, correct their papers, and go home without an upset stomach. They strive to present only those ideas or bits of information that are not controversial and hide from every ideological confrontation. They're just presenting "facts," just honing skills. In one sense at least, a great deal of information falls into such a "neutral" category. We are not going to engage in ideological combat, for example, when an astronomer tells us that the moon is 239 thousand miles away from the earth or that the earth's orbit around the sun takes 365 1/4 days to complete. We won't even object when he insists that the furthermost star detectable by telescope is billions of light years away from the planet earth. But when he insists that "the Big Bang" occurred approximately fifteen billion years ago and thereby created the universe as we know it, neutrality will be shattered and war will (or at least should) break out in the class-room. Defensive alignments will go into motion. Students worthy of the name begin to ponder some tough questions and spar with the professor in their efforts to prick his hot air theory. *What* went bang? *Where* and *when* did that something that went bang *originate?* What *caused* that mass of matter to explode? How is it possible for something subject to mass chaos to explode in such a way that the end product is characterized by the greatest possible precision and orderliness, such as our universe with all of its intricate orbits? When airplanes explode or when volcanoes erupt, the result is utter chaos. Why should a "Big Bang" be any different?

War should break out on such occasions, but it often doesn't. Students are often too timid, too defenseless, and too afraid of the people who control the grade book and the keys to their academic career. Students, too, prefer neutrality to war, especially when the instructor holds all the ammunition. In one sense, it is a shame that we waste education on the very young who are not yet ready to test the spirits, to see whether they are really in tune with the great hymnwriter of the universe. Instead of examining and analyzing the siren songs they hear, they often prefer to just sing along.

A classic case of persuasion is that of Horace Mann, secretary of the Massachusetts Board of Education for twelve years from 1837 to 1848. In an era when Calvinism was on the wane and liberalism on the rise, Mann proposed to have the public schools teach only that which was common to the various Protestant denominations, to have the Bible read without comment, and to have teachers by word and life illustrate nonsectarian Christianity.[33] Because he himself was a Unitarian, he fought with the zeal of the most ardent missionary and the cunning of the most clever politician to install a lowest-common-denominator religion in the Massachusetts schools. Forever pleading for peace, he fought until he finally won, until he persuaded all the opposition to lay down their pens and do things his way.

The "war" between the creation scientists and the theistic evolutionists is really not that much different. Both sides are using every arsenal at their disposal. Both sides are trying to capture the minds of their students and of the general public, in the hope that their perspective will be accepted. Both sides are exercising every power of persuasion that they can muster. Both sides are actors on the stage of the great antithesis, with each one claiming to be the rightful agents of the great Creator and King of the universe. For either side to claim neutrality is a sham and a ruse, a covert attempt to gain converts under the banner of peace.

In that great combat we all play a part. As students, we may not take on the role of a sponge, absorbing whatever comes our way. We are called to conflict, to choose this day whom we will serve, whether that be the God of the Scriptures, or the great pretender to His throne. As parents, we need to know what our children are being taught, whether that be through the television they watch, the books that they read, or the lectures to which they listen. As teachers, we have an especially heavy responsibility and need to remember that someday we will be called to account if we have led one little one astray. Because of our power to persuade, we need to pray each day that we teach them the truth and nothing but the truth. So help us, God.

CHAPTER FIVE

The Problem with Dating

DATING can be difficult. And confusing, too. A date is many different things. For one, it is a dried fruit that grows near the top of palm trees in desert country. For another, it is a social engagement between two people, usually of younger age and of the opposite sex. Those kinds of dating have their peculiar built-in problems. But those are not the kinds of dates about which I am concerned.

Dates are specific points of time on a calendar. We usually measure them in twenty-four hour segments, based on the rotation of the earth on its axis. January 1, we say, is a specific twenty-four hour period that is the same for everyone. It is a "fact" beyond dispute, a given within the world which God created. Furthermore, God created the entire universe within six of those twenty-four hour time segments and then set aside a seventh day for rest and worship.

Using such a mindset, God must have begun the work of creation on a Monday morning at precisely 12:01 A.M. in the year 4004 B.C. Since this is being written in the year of our Lord 1989, it can be concluded that the earth and the entire universe of which planet earth is a part, are approximately six thousand years old.

Such is the stuff of which arguments are made, most of them foolish. On the one side are those who are labelled as "literalists," those who adhere stridently to the chronology proposed by Bishop Usher in the seventeenth century and who insist that the days of creation, described for us in Genesis 1 and 2, are the twenty-four hour periods *as we know them*. Some of these literalists, whose publications help to fill my files, have computer printouts to prove their point. Some even go so far as to prescribe the month and day of that month on which God began His creative activity. Whenever I receive such literature, I am torn between the emotions of laughter and sadness. I want to cry because they have tried to prescribe such precise time restrictions to a God Who transcends all time, Who is and always was eternal. I want to laugh, on the other hand, because those time-bound creatures do not even question or claim to understand the times in which they are living. It seems as if for them, their timeframes are the heart of the Bible's message.

On the other side of the argument are those who want to insist that the earth is millions and even billions of years old. Those who advance this argument love to be labelled as "scientists" and scorn the conclusions reached by the "literalists" or "fundamentalist" Christians. Each side is convinced that the other is totally in the wrong, worthy of denunciation, and should be excluded from the privilege of teaching the next generation.

In order to work our way through the argument, often described, albeit mistakenly, as the core of the creation-evolution controversy, we need to examine carefully both sides of the issue and try to arrive at a Biblically defensible conclusion, based not on our presuppositions and assumptions, but on the clear teaching of God's Word. When such is done, it is quite possible that both sides are in the wrong, that both the "scientists" and the "literalists" have misread the Word and are guilty of distortion. The truth may not reside in either camp, but remain for us to discover afresh in the pages of Scripture. That is our task. It will not be simple or easy, but that is the road to wisdom, to which God himself calls us.

The Problem with Days

For almost twenty years now I have stubbornly refused to get involved in a debate with anyone about the meaning of the word "day" in Genesis. The reason is historical. On a given day I sat through a day-long (actually it was about six hours) symposium on the meaning of the word "day." I knew and trusted all the participants. All of them were Biblical scholars with excellent credentials from conservative, orthodox institutions. Each came armed with his Hebrew lexicon and his carefully selected passages of Scripture. Each one sounded most impressive in his presentation. But each one found it difficult to refute those who presented alternative viewpoints and interpretations. By the end of the day I was feeling like a used tennis ball and wondering if all the dialogue had even minutely restored my soul in its relationship to its Maker.

The question of "days" got another jolt more recently when I compared the text of the Westminster Confession with that of the Belgic Confession. The framers of the Westminster Standard, in their wisdom, saw fit to declare: "It pleased God . . . to create, or make of nothing, the world . . . in the space of six days."[34] Those who drafted the Belgic Confession, on the other hand, simply ignored the matter of days and declared that God had created the world "when it seemed good to Him."[35] As a denominational member who had long adhered to the latter creed, I could only conclude that, to my theological forbears, the matter of "days" was either problematic or inconsequential. After careful reflection, I have come to the conclusion that they are right.

When we approach the concept of "day," we need to remember that we usually come to the Scriptures with our preconceived, earth-bound, and provincial notion of time. We live in a culture that is regulated and almost obsessed by time. Clocks, though, are a relatively recent invention, and time zones were unheard of prior to the nineteenth century. Furthermore, we who live in North America think our technological precision must be imposed on the whole universe. We often forget that January 1 is really December 31 in Australia and that 3:00 P.M. in Los Angeles is really 6:00 P.M. in New York. Furthermore, we forget that a "day" on the earth is not the same length of time as a "day" on the moon or on any of the other planets. One of our "years" is but a small fraction of a "year" in the distant parts of our universe.

Since God created the entire universe "when it seemed good to Him," it is unwise on our part to insist that God used the twentieth century time frame of the planet earth when He created the universe. To make such insistence is to force God's actions and words into our culturally conditioned boxes.

Since the first two chapters of Genesis are central to the controversy, it is important that we examine them carefully. If we only look for specific references to "days," we will certainly find them. But if we read the entire chapters, we will also find exegetical difficulties.

Some Interpretation Problems[36]

24 Hour Days

Gen.

1.5   "God called the light 'day' and the darkness he called
        'night.' And there was evening, and there was morn-
        ing—the first day."

1.8   "And there was evening, and there was morning—the
        second day."

1.13   "And there was evening, and there was
        morning—the third day."

1.19   "And there was evening, and there was morning-the
        fourth day."

1.23   "And there was evening, and there was morning-the fifth
        day."

1.31   "And there was evening, and there was morning-the
        sixth day."

2.2   "By the seventh day God had finished the work he had
        been doing; so on the seventh day he rested from all his
        work."

1.6,7   "And God said, . . . And it was so." These phrases are
        repeated for each of the six days.

Ex.20.11

        "For in six days the Lord made the heavens and the
        earth, the sea, and all that is in them, but he rested on
        the seventh day."

Something Else

Gen.

1.2   "Now the earth was formless and empty, darkness was
        over the surface of the deep, and the Spirit of God was
        hovering over the waters."

N.B.   this text is the basis for the infamous "gap theory,"
        which argues that there was an indefinite time between
        Gen. 1.1 and 1.3.

1.11   *"Let the land produce* vegetation: seed-bearing plants
        and trees on the land."

1.12   *"The land produced* vegetation: plants bearing seed
        according to their kinds and trees bearing fruit with seed
        in it according to their kinds."

1.24 "Let *the land produce* living creatures according to their kinds: . . ."

2.4–7 "When the Lord God made the earth and the heavens, no shrub of the field had yet appeared on the earth and no plant of the field had yet sprung up; the Lord God had not sent rain on the earth and there was no man to work the ground, but streams came up from the earth and watered the whole surface of the ground. And the Lord God formed man from the dust of the ground . . ."

2.9 "And the Lord God made all kinds of trees *grow out of the ground . . .*"

2.19 "Now the Lord God *had formed out of the ground* all the beasts of the field and all the birds of the air."

Some Observations

1. If we insist on reading the text of Scripture in a strict *literalist* sense, we ought to do so with the complete creation account given to us in Genesis one and two, and not just with the phrases that reinforce our point of view.

2. By focusing on the underlined phrases in the second group, which are also part of God's infallible message, the reader could easily conclude that the creation process took longer than the 24 hour days as we know them.

3. By focusing primarily on the phrases in the first group, the reader would be inclined to conclude that God completed the entire creation in six twenty-four hour days.

4. If we call attention to the phraseology used in the second list, however, we run the risk of being accused of being "soft on evolution" or of giving the evolutionists ammunition to use against the creationists. Being true to Scripture, however, is more important than guarding our own reputations.

5. Given the assumptions that God cannot lie and that the entirety of Scripture is "useful for teaching, rebuking, correcting, and training in righteousness" (II Tim. 3:16), we may need to conclude that the precise chronology of the creation account is either not important or not the primary message that God is revealing to us in the first two chapters of Genesis.

6. Reading the Genesis account with attention to both the left-hand and the right-hand columns should *not* lead one to conclude that they are mythical, primeval, nor "mere packaging," as some are wont to do. They are still wholly truthful, historical, and factual about the events there described. What one can conclude is that they are not totally detailed or chronologically specific in the sense that a blueprint or construction contract would be. Such is not the intent or purpose of God's Word.

There is always the danger that we approach a text, any text, with the intent of finding there reinforcement for our core beliefs or our favorite presuppositions. When we do that, we force the text to say what we want it to say. We do that with Scripture, too, attempting thereby to put words into God's mouth and using Him for our advantage. We see God as our mouthpiece rather than seeing ourselves as His disciples.

My own conclusion, after repeated and careful study of the Genesis account, is that the precise chronology of God's creative acts and/or processes ought not be our central concern. God in His wisdom has seen fit not to give us that kind of precise detail and seems to have deliberately withheld it from us. Maybe someday, when we are restored to the pre-fall perfection enjoyed by Adam and Eve, we will also understand that clearly. For now, we see it darkly, as through a glass.

The Genealogies

The sum of the argument, however, does not rest on the meaning of the word "day." If that were the case, those who wish to contest the Biblical account of creation ought to content themselves with criticizing only chapters one and two of Genesis and leave the remaining chapters out of consideration. But the advocates of evolutionary theory insist on expanding their reinterpretation to chapters three through eleven. They insist that all of Genesis 1–11 must be classified as prehistoric myth or primeval story.

There is good reason for such insistence. Those who adamantly demand acceptance of evolutionary theory want to dispense with both the Noahic flood and the genealogies from Adam to Abraham. The flood, after all, is the antithesis of their wholly unsubstantiated ice age theory and must be discounted completely if there is to be acceptance for its substitute. At the same time, the very precise chronologies of Genesis 5 and 11 must be eliminated if one is to accept the notion of pre-Adamic man and an "old" earth.

But the Bible is plain and capable of being understood even by very young children. Since many people have never taken time to read or study the genealogies so clearly detailed in Scripture, they are presented here.

Genealogical Tables

Gen.5	*Elapsed Time*	*I Chron. 1*	*Luke 3*
Adam	130	Adam	Adam
Seth	105	Seth	Seth
Enosh	90	Enosh	Enosh
Kenan	70	Kenan	Kenan
Mahalalel	65	Mahalalel	Mahalalel
Jared	162	Jared	Jared
Enoch	65	Enoch	Enoch
Methuselah	187	Methuselah	Methuselah
Lamech	182	Lamech	Lamech
Noah	502	Noah	Noah
Gen. 11			
Shem	98	Shem	Shem
Arphaxad	35	Arphaxad	Arphaxad
Shelah	30	Shelah	Cainan*
Eber	34	Eber	Shelah
Peleg	30	Peleg	Eber
Reu	32	Reu	Peleg
Serug	30	Serug	Reu
Nahor	29	Nahor	Serug
Terah	70	Terah	Nahor
Abram		Abram	Terah
			Abraham
Total	1946		

Note: 1. If we accept these chapters as divinely inspired revelation, the flood occurred in the six hundreth year of Noah's life when Shem was ninety-eight years old (Gen. 7: 11, 8:13, 9:28, 11:10), or 1,656 years after the creation of Adam. From our vantage point we could conclude that the Noahic flood occurred some twenty-three hundred to twenty-four hundred years before the birth of Christ.

2. Abram was born 292 years after the flood, or 1,946 years after Adam was created (see Gen. 11:10–27).

When one stops to study the Scriptural accounts of these genealogies, one is struck by various factors. The first is that these lists of names follow a very precise line or branch of the family tree of mankind. Only one branch of each generation is chosen, and that for a very particular reason. The primary purpose is to point to Christ. The entire Bible, from Genesis to Revelation, is Christo-centric. As soon as Adam and Eve sinned, God promised them a Savior (Gen. 3:15). Each of the three genealogic accounts is an overt exercise by the author of Scripture to link the first Adam with the second Adam. The primary purpose of the Bible then, is the redemption of God's chosen people. It is *redemptive* history, but it is also *history*.

A second observation that needs to be made is that there is almost total harmony between the accounts as given to us in Genesis, Chronicles, and Luke. In Luke's genealogy there is the unexplained occurrence of Cainan between Arphaxad and Shelah,[37] but apart from that there is complete agreement. This harmony becomes significant, especially when we consider the alternative of either accepting or rejecting God's Word.[38]

A third observation is that the lineage from Adam to Abraham is *chronologically precise*. The Bible gives us not only the exact number of years that each patriarch lived, but also tells us the precise age of the father at the time the son was born. This is true not only in one version, but in all the versions used by the Christian church. On this point, then, all the ancient manuscripts and all the modern-day versions are in agreement. Simple arithmetic or twentieth century computers will yield the same results. From the creation of Adam, the dates of the Noahic flood and the birth of Abram can be easily measured. Any "scientist" can count those numbers as often as he wants, but the outcome will always be the same. The conclusion, therefore, should be obvious: the first Adam is of relatively recent creation.

Two Alternatives

The above conclusion is obvious to me and may also be to the reader, but there are millions of people who will strongly protest. The objection, even amongst many Christians, is that the first eleven chapters of Genesis cannot be read as history. They are simply not factually correct, they say. The entire period before Abraham is to be classified as prehistoric or primeval history or mythology. Anyone who finally gets pushed off the proverbial fence and admits to being an evolutionist will refuse to accept the historicity of Genesis 1–11. Such rejection will come, not because of careful exegesis of the Biblical text, but because that person has been culturally conditioned to reject the clear teaching of Scripture. He has been taught by parents, by historians, by biologists, by anthropologists, by geologists, and even by theologians to call into question the veracity of Genesis 1–11. Given that kind of conditioning, the reaction is predictable: those prehistoric myths may be very interesting, but they certainly are not true.

It would be very easy to get lost in all the detailed arguments which have been advanced over the centuries against these first eleven chapters of the Bible, but we ultimately must confront one simple option: Do we believe God's Word as true, or do we reject it as false? Do we accept God's account, or do we accept the accounts of those who want to preach evolution? Do we call God a liar or do we call Satan a liar?

The one who rejects the first eleven chapters of Genesis cannot stop there. If he doesn't agree with Genesis 5 and 11, he must be consistent and also reject the books of Chronicles, Matthew, and Luke. In addition, he must reject all those other references by the prophets, by Christ, and by the apostles to the events recorded in Genesis 1–11. As Ken Ham has so capably illustrated, an attack on Genesis is an attack on all of Scripture.[39] If you undermine the foundation, the building will soon fall.

Telescopic Dating

Just yesterday my barber asked me what I was writing now. When I told her that the subject was the creation-evolution controversy, she stopped cutting and peppered me with questions. "I suppose you still believe that the earth is six thousand years old," she asked. When I replied that that was probably a reasonable ballpark figure, her jaw dropped in disbelief.

Some of my more schooled acquaintances have an even more vigorous reaction. They are quick to denounce such calculations as uninformed, unscientific, and worthy of acceptance only by "fundamentalists" and "literalists." They quickly appeal to the likes of Carl Sagan and Howard Van Til as authorities who have *proven* the earth to be much older. They also appeal to their high school science teachers and to the encyclopedia on their shelves.

One person who has pushed the age of the earth to its farthest limits is Howard Van Til, author of *The Fourth Day*. Purporting to be an evangelical Christian, he has claimed that the earth is at least 14.5 billion years old.[40] He has objected stridently to every argument for a young earth and has claimed that "Bringing questions about . . . cosmic chronology to the Bible is simply inappropriate to its very character and purposes. The study of the . . . temporal development of the cosmos is exclusively and exhaustively the domain of the natural sciences."[41]

But how could Van Til and Biblical "literalists" be so far apart? How could one Christian come to the conclusion that the earth is somewhat more than six thousand years old, while the other claims that it is somewhere in the range of 14.5 to 15 billion? The answer is simple: one uses *Biblical* dating while the other uses *telescopic* dating.

Howard Van Til is an astronomer and an astrophysicist. His primary object of study is the universe of planets and stars. His primary tool for research is the telescope. He looks through the telescopes that are available to him or reads the accounts of others who have looked through telescopes. The farthest star known to man is 14.5 billion light years distant from the earth. Since it would take, by their computer calculations, 14.5 billion years for that light to travel from that star to earth, the earth must be at least that old. Simple. The argument is closed until we discover, by use of a more powerful telescope, an even more distant star. When that happens, we will simply increase the age of the earth.

But wait! Something is missing.

Apparent Age

Wrapped up in Van Til's argument is a very significant presupposition. He *assumes* that God could not and would not create a star with light emanating from it. He *assumes* a creation without any apparent age. He finds the "apparent-age concept to be entirely un-acceptable because it requires God's creation to be more of an illu-sion than a reality."[42] He goes on to assert that "the apparent-age concept . . . transforms the Creator of a coherent cosmos into a divine magician—a master of the deceptive art of illusion."[43]

If Van Til were at the wedding in Cana of Galilee, he probably would also have been fooled by the water turned to wine. Not only would the miraculous process have violated the naturalistic laws he understands, but he also would have been fooled by the apparent age of that which the guests decided was the best of the feast.

This fundamental assumption has not been the focus of much discussion, but it ought to be. Those who argue for an old earth could not arrive at their conclusions without first holding to that presupposition. The assumption, however, is seriously flawed. First of all, it imposes tight restrictions on God's creative activity. Second, such restrictions are nothing less than covert warnings to God that He may not fool us. But who are we to demand that God confine Himself to those actions and processes which are under-standable and acceptable to our sin-warped minds? Such a mindset demands that the Creator comply with our theory of evolutionary origins. Third, it eliminates the possibility of creation. Let me ex-plain.

To say that nothing could have apparent age at the time of crea-tion would be equivalent to saying that nothing could be created. Everything has the appearance of age. If we could visualize that distant star of which Van Til speaks, and find that there was no light projecting from it, we would either fail to recognize it as a star or conclude that it was too young to produce light. When God created a tree, a dog, a flower, or Adam, that object had some size, shape, and form to it. If we had been there to analyze it, we would have concluded that it *appeared* to have some age, whether that be two hours, two weeks, two months, or twenty years. To take away all *appearance* of age would require that we reduce it to the original, single cell from which it was conceived. But even that cell, when examined microscopically, would have some apparent age.

None of us were there, of course, but a created world of planets, stars, animals, and plants, all of which had no appearance of age, is simply inconceivable. Van Til and others may have difficulty accepting the concept of apparent age, but the alternative is worse. To allow for nothing to have the appearance of age is to allow for nothing to exist.

Radiometric Dating

In the history of evolutionary theory the concept of radiometric or carbon-dating is even more widespread. Those who specialize in biology, chemistry, and geology put their stock in the accuracy of the radiometric-dating process. Without going into detail of how they supposedly measure the age of fossils, rocks, skeletons, and geologic strata, we need to call attention to the basic assumption or presupposition on which these calculations rest. That assumption is one we have analyzed before.[44] It is called the uniformitarian principle, or uniformitarianism.

Geologists measure the age of the earth by examining a given object and determining how much it disintegrates over a given period of time. The time period is always relatively brief, since no one has decades or centuries to observe the decomposition of a sedimentary rock or a dinosaur bone. Regardless of the length of time devoted to the study, no one can approach the actual or historic time for total decay. What everyone does, then, is to extrapolate backwards through time to arrive at an approximate age for that object. This approach to dating goes back to the work of Charles Lyell, whose writings we discussed earlier. What almost every geologist since has *assumed* is that the rate of decay has always been consistent. Uniformity of rate and process are essential to their calculations.

What these evolutionists refuse to allow is the possibility that the Noahic flood was a real historic event. The calactysmic events described for us in Genesis 6–8, if allowed to stand, would wreak havoc with all their calculations and throw their uniformitarian assumptions on the academic trash pile.

The conflict, then, is between those who accept the Biblical account of the flood and those who, in blind faith, adhere to the teachings of Charles Lyell. Alan Dundes, editor of *The Flood Myth,* recognized the conflict clearly. Although he devoted all his efforts to a rejection of the "flood myth," he was astute enough to recognize that, "If the historicity of the flood could be maintained, . . . then the Bible itself as a bastion of Christian faith could remain safe and intact."[45]

What evolutionists perpetually (and quietly) do is set up their presuppositions as the screen through which the Word of God must be filtered. Whatever will not meet the criteria of uniformitarianism must be rejected. Genesis 1–11 fails their test.

A Fatal Obsession

Within the Christian community there are always some people wanting to predict the time of Christ's second coming. Sporadically one will hear about some person or other who gives a precise day and year on which the end of the world will occur. To date, they have all been wrong. There are others who make eschatology (the doctrine of the end times) the primary focus of their gospel message. To them Christ has been very emphatic: "No one knows about that day or hour, not even the angels in heaven, nor the Son, but only the Father."[46]

What is stunning about this statement is Jesus' admission that even He did not know when the end would come. He did, however, know that there was going to be a final day and warned His listeners to be ready at all times. For each of us, that end may come tomorrow.

On the other end of time, namely, the beginning of earth's history, we note an even greater obsession with the dating of earth's origin. Christians and non-Christians alike have long been concerned with dating the world. There is nothing wrong or inherently evil in that concern, but there is something wrong when that develops into an obsession.

Those who teach and do research in the areas of biology, chemistry, or geology have no need to be concerned with writing history. Yet they stubbornly persist in pretending to be historians. Some of them, like Carl Sagan and Stephen Gould, expend most of their energies outside their own self-imposed "scientific" boundaries and insist on writing the history of the universe.

EVOLUTIONISTS' OBSESSION
WITH WRITING HISTORY

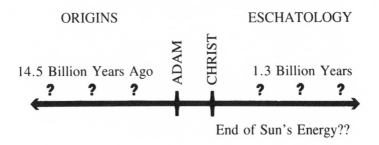

ORIGINS   ESCHATOLOGY

ADAM   CHRIST

14.5 Billion Years Ago   1.3 Billion Years

?   ?   ?   ?   ?   ?

End of Sun's Energy??

Based on uniformitarian principles, evolutionists have decided that the history of the earth extends back at least 14.5 billion years (14,500,000,000). If those same uniformitarian principles were applied to the future, when would the end occur? Would there ever be a final judgment?

Earlier in this chapter we made some specific observations about the dating of the Noahic flood and about the birth of Abram. In doing so, we consciously related both events to Christ, for that is the primary focus of Scripture. We can arrive at such conclusions because God gives us precise genealogical tables within His Word by which to make those calculations. What we cannot do, however, is arrive at any specific date of the origin of the universe, for that God has seen fit not to reveal.[47]

Throughout the nineteenth and twentieth centuries there have been persistent efforts by evolutionists to peg the earth's origin at progressively earlier dates. Whereas a few million years was enough to satisfy earlier advocates, now billions of years have become the standard. In theistic and atheistic circles alike, the dating game has become a *fatal* obsession. It will be fatal because it is an overt attempt to *disprove* the teachings of God's holy Word. In the language of Ken Ham, evolution is a lie. It is a conscious, deliberate effort to destroy the credibility of Genesis 1–11 and to replace it with a mechanistic view of the universe in which God is confined by naturalistic processes. The Creator is no longer the Sovereign Architect Who must answer to no one, but a mere puppet Who must respond to man's finite wishes. Such rejection the jealous God of the Bible will not ignore.

The Wisdom of Job

"In the land of Uz there lived a man whose name was Job. This man was blameless and upright; he feared God and shunned evil . . . He was the greatest man among all the peoples of the East."[48] Throughout the history of the Judaic-Christian tradition, Job has been considered as one of the wisest men ever to have lived.

Yet at the conclusion of the book the Lord comes to that wise man and asks,

Who is this that darkens my counsel
with words without knowledge?

Brace yourself like a man;
  I will question you,
and you shall answer me.[49]

With such an introduction, God begins to pepper Job almost mercilessly with questions. Throughout four chapters (38–41) God throws at Job query after query about the creation of the world. Were you there? Do you even begin to understand? Do you dare to correct the Almighty? Will you condemn me to justify yourself? Can you set up God's dominion over the earth?

Finally, humbly, Job replies:

> I know that you can do all things; no plan of yours can be thwarted.
> You asked, "Who is this that obscures my counsel without knowledge?"
> Surely I spoke of things I did not understand,
> Things too wonderful for me to know.[50]

That must be our response, too. The creation of the universe in all of its mind-boggling dimensions is beyond our most enlightened visions. Ours is not to figure how or even when, but to praise and worship the One Who said, "Let there be."

CHAPTER SIX
God's Wedding Band

A pot of gold at the end of the rainbow! That picture adorns numerous ads for state lottery jackpots. Because of it, countless people are only too anxious to plunk down another one, two, ten, or twenty dollars as an investment in their future. The imagery is powerful, even though the odds would dictate that a rathole would be an equally safe investment.

On a more mundane but more honest level, a rainbow is an arc of colors seen against a sunlit sky when droplets of water are in the air. We see them most often when a rainstorm has moved off to the east in the evening hours, but we also catch them when sunlight plays off a waterfall, a lawn sprinkler, or even a soap bubble.

Rainbows are beautiful to behold, with their mixtures of red, orange, yellow, green, blue, and violet colors. Sometimes they send us into ecstasy and cause us to scurry for our cameras, only to find that modern photography does not do justice to what we actually saw. Somehow our film cannot capture the full glory and excitement of that band of colors in the sky.

A couple of years ago I was flabbergasted, though, by a picture of a rainbow. It was taken from high in the air over the islands of Hawaii. A photographer in an airplane captured on film something I had never seen before. It was a perfectly circular rainbow! No ends softly brushing against the horizon. No pot of gold. In fact, no ends! Just a beautiful round ring.

A little over a year ago my wife and I saw one ourselves. In the flesh, you might say. We were flying from Chicago to Boston, cruising at some thirty thousand feet. Occupying a window seat, as I always try to do, I spotted a beauty, cast against a bank of clouds that were well below us and off to the left. We wanted the pilot to stop for a photo session, but he was oblivious to our desire and to our theological sensitivity. So we raced on. That glorious rainbow was soon out of sight, but not out of mind.

Physicists might be inclined to recognize that rainbows are really perfect circles, when the whole of them can be seen. But no mere study of physics can explain the meaning or the significance of those circular shapes. Our earth-bound feet are planted too firmly in a study of general revelation. Our finite vision is limited by our angles and the limiting horizons which seem to smother those rings of splendor into the hillsides.

When we study Scripture, however, a whole new picture comes into focus. When viewed through the spectacles of God's special revelation, the rainbow takes on new, amazing dimensions, and looks more and more like a wedding ring. Let me explain.

We first read about the rainbow in Gen. 9:13, where God says, "I have set my rainbow in the clouds, and it will be the sign of the covenant between me and the earth." That verse, and the ones immediately following, are pregnant with multiple meanings, only a few of which can be explained here. For now, we want to focus primarily on the rainbow and what it means.

In order to understand the significance of the rainbow, we need to go back in history to the time before the flood. And God sent the flood because He was angry at the sinful condition in His creation. Genesis 6:5 tells us that, "the Lord saw how great man's wickedness on the earth had become, and that every inclination of the thoughts of his heart was only evil all the time." Sin and its consequences had become so rampant that God "was grieved that He had made man on the earth, and His heart was filled with pain" (vs. 6).

At least sixteen hundred years had passed since God had created Adam and Eve and they had succumbed to Satan's tempting arguments. Over the centuries, men and women had become exceedingly evil. God was both angry and sad. His beautiful creatures and creation had become sinful and sour.

In His righteous fury, God sent such a devastating flood that "every living thing that moved on the earth perished—birds, livestock, wild animals, and all mankind. Everything on dry land that had the breath of life in its nostrils died" (7:21–2). "Only Noah was left, and those with him in the ark" (vs. 23).

That is the background. But when we get to Genesis 9, the flood is history. The waters have receded, the oceans have settled into their new boundaries, and all the creatures preserved in the ark once again have their feet on terra firma. Whereas chapters 6 and 7 emphasized the justice of God, chapters 8 and 9 call attention to his covenant faithfulness. God is not only righteous and holy; He is also loving and compassionate. Man, after all, had been created in God's own likeness. God, therefore, comes to Noah and his family with the terms and promise of a beautiful covenant.

The Noahic covenant is, among other things, comprehensive. The agreement, God says, is between "me *and the earth*." "Never again will all life be cut off by the waters of a flood; never again will there be a flood to destroy the earth" (9:11). The promise is also noteworthy because it is God-originated. God, in His love and mercy, recites for Noah's family a promise of faithfulness and enduring love. But, even more striking, the sign of the covenant, the rainbow, is a reminder *to God Himself*. The rainbow will appear after the rain, not as a reminder to man, but as a reminder to God. "Whenever I bring clouds over the earth and the rainbow appears in the clouds, *I will remember* my covenant" (9:14–15). Then, for emphasis, the promise is repeated, "*I will see it and remember* the everlasting covenant" (vs.16).

But why does God need such constant reminders?

When we sit back and reflect on such a significant question, we need to recall that God has a different vantage point, a different perspective on His creation than we do. He looks at it from the top down. We look at it from the bottom up. We look at the rainbow and see only a fraction of it. When the sun is at an angle greater than forty-two degrees, we do not see the rainbow at all. We see it extending only from one part of the horizon to another. But God sees it in its entirety, all the time.

But there is an even more important reason why God gave the rainbow as a reminder to Himself. God, after all, is our husband. We are His bride. And the rainbow is a wedding ring. It is the seal and sign of our marriage, given to us and His whole creation, that we are henceforth united to Him in a bond of holy wedlock.

Such language may seem strange at first, but it ought not surprise us. In numerous New Testament passages Christ is referred to as the bridegroom, and the church is His bride. But already in the Old Testament there are countless references to Israel's sin being that of adultery, which is a violation of marriage vows.

One of the most poignant characterizations of this marriage relationship is given to us by the prophet Isaiah:

"For your maker is your husband—the Lord Almighty is his name . . . The Lord will call you back as if you were a wife deserted . . . . a wife who married young, only to be rejected," says your God. "For a brief moment I abandoned you, but with deep compassion I will bring you back . . . . To me this is like the days of Noah, when I swore that the waters of Noah would never again cover the earth. So now I have sworn not to be angry with you, never to rebuke you again" (54:5–9).

Those of us who are married wear wedding bands. We wear them, not to remind our spouses that they are married to us, but that we are married to them. In that respect, God is no different. From His vantage point, the rainbow is a never-ending circle, a marvelous reminder that He is married to us and to His creation. The rainbow is His wedding band. The next time you get up in the air, look around. You just might see it too.

Epilogue

IT is no secret that there is a significant difference between the theory of theistic evolution and that of scientific creationism. These two camps, both avowing Christianity, and both appealing for support from Christians, are unalterably opposed to each other. Both claim that their reading of Scripture is correct and that the other's is seriously flawed.

Throughout the preceding chapters I have attempted to analyze and dissect this controversy, not from an attitude of feigned neutrality, but from the vantage point of Biblical creationism. By faith I accept the Scriptures as the Word of God, divinely authored and fully reliable. By faith, then, I reject that which does not harmonize with the clear and obvious teaching of those Scriptures.

Evolution falls into the latter category. Evolution, though, comes in at least two varieties. On the one hand there is the atheistic or naturalistic version popularized by Charles Darwin, Carl Sagan, and Stephen Gould. All of us, as Christians, are unequivocally out of harmony with that strain. The second variety, that of theistic evolution, or creationomic science, as Howard Van Til prefers to call it, is a more difficult problem to address. It is problematic because there are countless Christian colleagues, friends, and even blood relatives who have been persuaded of its authenticity. Families, congregations, and denominations are tearing at each other either in defense of or in opposition to it.

Theistic evolution did not just happen and it will not soon disappear. Like Topsy, it just grew and grew in response to a wide array of cultural conditions, mushrooming during the 1970s and 1980s to a point where it has overshadowed traditional creationism.

Every idea has consequences, but every idea also has its origins or roots. It does not blossom in thin air, but has its genesis in the soil of intellectual history. So, too, with theistic evolution. The diagram below will give us a simplified version of that intellectual history, with only the major roots being identified.

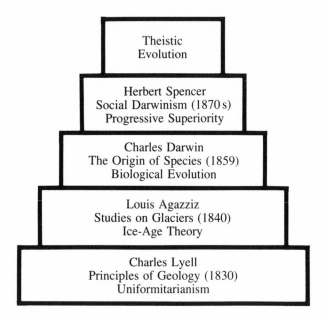

For those who have read the preceding chapters closely, it will be apparent that the author has not dealt in any significant fashion with either the works of Herbert Spencer or Charles Darwin. Suffice it to say that it was the work of Spencer that made the writing of Darwin palatable to the public taste. By taking Darwin's ideas about survival of the fittest and applying them to society at large, he appealed to our egos and left us believing that each generation is more intelligent than the last. That is a powerful concept, imbibed by the vast majority of Western students, and unquestioned by all except the astute. Without Spencer's ideas clearing out the opposition, it is doubtful whether *The Origin of Species* would be well known today.

The writings of Darwin have not occupied a prominent place on these pages either. That should never be construed to mean that he is unimportant and should not be carefully critiqued. On the contrary, I think every teacher assigned to the discipline of biology should assess his writings and coerce his students to test *The Origin of Species* against the rules of logic and the rigors of academic proof. I have no doubt that the book will fail miserably, as many naturalistic evolutionists have begrudgingly admitted. Also, since so many scholars, more capable than I, have dissected Darwin's writings, there is little point in my repeating their analyses here.

What I have attempted is an examination of those foundational concepts on which the writings of all theistic evolutionists and of Darwin rest. Specifically, I have addressed the ice-age theory initiated by Louis Agazziz and the principle of uniformitarianism enunciated by Charles Lyell. The ice-age or glacial epoch theory in particular has come in for intensive scrutiny because it has historically been a substitute for the cataclysmic flood described for us in Genesis 6-10. For those who want to reject the flood account, it is imperative that the historicity of those first chapters in Genesis be challenged. Since they cannot be totally eliminated from the canon of Scripture, the next best thing is to characterize them as myth, fable, folk-tale, or literary packaging.

The power of water in large quantities is awesome. Even a small localized flood caused by four or five inches of rain can cause irreparable alteration to the landscape. When such is magnified to world-wide dimensions, with water covering the highest mountains, the potential alterations to topography boggle our imaginations. Yet that is precisely what God Himself tells us happened. To deny His Word or to reinterpret it to fit our own theories is to call Him a liar.

But God does not and cannot lie. He alone is truth. He alone is all-powerful and all-knowing. In contrast to Him, those who reject His Word and those who substitute their own fanciful explanations are the real liars. The glacial epoch theory, first espoused by Agazziz and enlarged by his disciples, is a blatant lie, a distortion of the truth. If falsehoods were rated on a scale of one to ten, it would deserve a unanimous ten.

Those are strong charges, I know. To further demonstrate the validity of those accusations, the reader is asked to ponder the following statements from *Geology Illustrated* by John Shelton.[51]

Geology was not a science until the legendary "Noachian" flood and six-day creation were replaced by explanations derived from careful study of rocks. The doctrine that past events should be explainable through no more than reasonable extensions of observable processes has played a vital role in substituting the plausible for the preposterous and the feasible for the fanciful in geology (p.351).

Even in today's most arid part of the Great Basin there is widespread evidence not only of former lakes but also of connecting rivers. The view in Figure 337 shows part of one of the many gorges cut by such rivers in the southern part of the Great Basin. Only a powerful stream working rather rapidly could produce such steep walls, yet these canyons are now either dry or contain only an intermittent trickle (p.356).

The fact that shoreline features are rather well preserved throughout the Great Basin, even when developed on loose sand and gravel, has led all who have studied them to conclude that they are geologically quite recent. But the likely hypothesis that they are in some way connected with the Pleistocene Ice Age is more difficult to prove and refine than one might think (p.360).

The result was an enormous five-pronged Pleistocene lake centered near Missoula, Montana, which filled Bitterroot, Blackfoot, Flathead, and numerous other valleys. Shorelines, beach deposits, and deltas show that its surface was about 4,150 feet above sea level, 1,000 feet above Missoula, and 2,000 feet above Spokane. This great body of water, glacial Lake Missoula, had a total area of about 2,990 square miles, a maximum depth of 2,000 feet, and an estimated volume of over 500 cubic miles, held in by ice at the west and north and by mountains on the east and south.

Ice dams are not permanent. The breakup of this one left abundant evidence of the flood it released. At various places along the Clark Fork in western Montana, leading to the outlet of glacial Lake Missoula, there are gravel bars bearing giant ripples up to 50 feet high and as much as 500 feet from crest to crest. Where the flow was constricted by narrows, the steep valley walls are swept conspicuously clean up to more than 1,000 feet above the valley floor. These gravel bars and clean valley walls are taken as evidence that the lake emptied suddenly when the ice dam gave way. Calculations suggest that the discharge may have reached a maximum of over 9 cubic miles per hour—1,900 times the average flow of the Colorado River in the Grand Canyon and well over 100 times flood stage on the lower Mississippi. Such a discharge probably lasted only a few days; at half the estimated maximum discharge, the available water would have drained out in three days. The flood would have stopped almost as abruptly as it started (pp.350–351).

Notice in the first quotation that Shelton there describes the Genesis flood as "legendary," "preposterous," and "fanciful." The glacial epoch theory, on the other hand, he characterizes as "reasonable," "observable," "plausible," and "feasible." By such pejorative language, the unwary might be persuaded. But note what follows.

Shelton, after rejecting the Genesis flood, invents his own. The evidences for a flood are overwhelming, especially in the Great Basin of the mountainous West. Even Shelton, an unabashed evolutionist, can see them plainly, so he calls attention to numerous features that could only have been carved by enormous amounts of water rushing to reach their own level. But then he invents "ice dams," high in the mountains, large enough for their breakup to carve out the numerous, monstrous canyons that dot the West! Not once, but numerous times! Over millions of years, with millions and even billions of years intervening, these great glaciers formed and then receded. No matter that such massive glaciation goes contrary to all the uniformitarian principles articulated by Charles Lyell. No matter that glaciers are simply frozen water which somehow had to accumulate at levels equal to or greater than that described by God in the book of Genesis. No matter that all the observable evidence demands a flood; we will simply substitute an ice pack and hope that the reader will not notice.

Conclusion

God is a merciful Father, a marvelous Creator, and an angry Judge. In His righteous fury, He caused "all the springs of the great deep

[to] burst forth, and the floodgates of the heavens [to be] opened."[52] But He also is the One Who, out of compassion for His creation and love for His image-bearers, set the rainbow in the sky and Who promised, "Never again will the waters become a flood to destroy all life."[53] Finally, out of an unending love for His bride, the church of Jesus Christ, He reminded them,

> For your Maker is your husband—the Lord Almighty is his name—the Holy One of Israel is your Redeemer; He is called the God of all the earth.

> To me this is like the days of Noah, when I swore that the waters of Noah would never again cover the earth. So now I have sworn not to be angry with you, never to rebuke you again.[54]

> Whenever the rainbow appears in the clouds, I will see it and remember the everlasting covenant between God and all living creatures of every kind on the earth.[55]

God's wedding band. What a reminder.

Appendix A
A Case in Point

IN the foregoing chapters I have attempted to share with the reader what I believe to be a Biblical perspective on the creation-evolution controversy. That battle has been assaulting our sensibilities for the past one hundred and fifty years. Some of us are growing weary of it, especially when the strongest clashes have involved professing Christians on both sides.

I have tried to alter the tone and direction of the conflict by focusing on the central teachings of Scripture and calling attention to the importance of training our nation's youth so that they can effectively "test the spirits" of our age. In the process, I have drawn an either/or position which could conceivably result in both sets of protagonists rasping for rebuttal. I hope not.

Although the action of large masses of ice may have played a role in terminal stages of the flood, those who see the Biblical deluge as the primary geologic agent, depositing fossils and shaping the present crust of the earth, must reject the theory that huge glaciers advanced ever so slowly from the poles and then retreated through several cycles of equally long interglacial periods. In that sense, at least, there must be an either/or proposition.

As an illustration of how this either/or position could work out in practice, consider the following case in point. One of my original efforts in sorting out the salient elements of this controversy resulted in the publication of an article entitled "Ice or Water?" Shortly after its appearance, a rather critical reply was received from Dr. Clarence Menninga, a professor of geology at my alma mater. He rejected my formulation of the problem and thus began a series of replies, included here for the reader's perusal.

Which side is right? Who won the debate? I'll let you, the reader, decide. Enjoy yourself.

Ice or Water

If you had a choice, which would you prefer, ice or water? On a hot July afternoon I might prefer the ice, which, I know, will soon turn to water anyway. On a cold December morning I would probably alter my choice, since it is easier to make a steaming cup of coffee with something that isn't frozen solid.

Such choices are trivial when limited to the palate and need not long concern us. But there is another, more profound choice when it comes to curricular materials for our schools. The options again are between ice and water, but now on massive, historic scales that will affect the worldview of generations yet unborn.

The question we all need to address is whether textbooks should present the perspective of a glacial epoch (a great Ice Age) or a Noahic flood. Numerous books that I have consulted give us that choice, but almost never in the same book. From the lowest elementary to the college level, one can find social studies, history, geography, and natural science texts that argue in favor of glaciation as the primary factor in shaping and determining the earth's crust and form. These books, sometimes obliquely and sometimes blatantly, perpetuate the notion that most of the northern hemisphere at one time was covered with ice. Huge glaciers, 10,000 to 15,000 feet thick, slowly, methodically crept down from the north pole regions and then as deliberately retreated, with the last one leaving Wisconsin less than twelve thousand years ago.

When I sit in classrooms observing our teachers or review the latest curricular materials, such "scientific" descriptions raise their ugly heads at varying levels, just waiting to be challenged. Regrettably, few teachers rise to the occasion, but let them pass as though here were another indisputable fact of science. Most teachers, in fact, are excessively naive and gullible when it comes to glacial theory and do not know how to critique it when it appears in their textbooks. Therefore, this article.

The foundation for a great Ice Age or Glacial Epoch theory was first articulated by Louis Agassiz (1807–73) who became fascinated by glaciers in the Swiss Alps. He drilled a series of holes in a glacier, planted flags in the holes, and then noted the gradual movement over a period of time. He also noted that the glacier receded as the weather warmed and left varying types of pulverized sediment in its wake. In 1840 he published his first book on the subject and entitled it *Etudes sur les Glaciers* (*Studies on Glaciers*). Six years later he moved to the United States, took a position at Harvard, and soon discovered similar-looking sedimentary deposits in this country. For a variety of unknown reasons, many of Agassiz's disciples focused their attention on the beautiful state of Wisconsin. Claiming to have found numerous evidences of glaciers there, they advanced the theory that most of Canada and the United States at one time had been covered with massive glaciers, extending as far south as Arkansas and the Ohio River.

According to this imaginatively crafted mythology, somewhere around one million years ago there developed a period of excessive snowfall which never melted, but turned into massive ice floes, and which kept pushing further and further south, crushing, grinding, scarring, and pulverizing everything in their path. In Europe and Asia the theorists argued, the glaciers extended as far southward as the Mediterranean and Caspian Seas.

Wisconsin remains as one focal point of presumed glacial evidence for many who hold blind faith in the Ice Age theory. The beautiful Wisconsin

Dells, for example, came into being because the "old" river was filled with glacial sediment, so a "new" river had to be carved in a presumably softer section of the earth's crust. Kettle Moraine State Park is another "proof" that is offered, as are the thousands of small, shallow lakes that were scooped out as the glacier moved southward. Niagara Falls, with its deep cut through the escarpment was also explained as a "new" river forced into existence by glaciated filling of the old. In order to give credibility to the theory of a glacial epoch, Charles Lyell hypothesized that the rate of erosion at Niagara Falls was one foot per year, thus allowing for the vast time spans that the theory required. Recent observations at the Falls, however, give the rate of erosion at five feet per year, but Lyell's timetable is still vigorously defended by those who blindly believe.

Everyone knows that it would be unwise to argue against glaciers as such. Anyone who has traveled to the Canadian Rockies or the Alps would readily admit that glaciers exist and have certain distinct qualities. They move slowly, by gravitational pull, from higher to lower elevations. They increase their size during the cold winter months and progressively melt as the weather gets warmer. The lower the temperature and the greater the snowfall, the larger the glacier. That is the nature of water turned to snow and ice.

It is quite another thing, however, to conclude that because glaciers currently exist at high mountain elevations, they must therefore have covered North America from Long Island to Denver and from Hudson Bay to Saint Louis. Such a conclusion defies all scientific explanation and requires logical leaps of the greatest magnitude.

If it is presumed that the existence of similar sediment in Wisconsin and Switzerland requires the existence of earth-covering glaciers, then it would be as logical to conclude that Volvos and Toyotas were all made by General Motors. Such blind, illogical leaps of faith would also allow me to conclude that because I found ice in both my refrigerator and in Glacier National Park, both originated in my kitchen.

When Agassiz's disciples first postulated the Glacial Epoch theory, there was a storm of protest and criticism. Those who held to traditional Judeo-Christian teachings were quick to realize that their theory was a poorly conceived substitute for the Noahic flood. They, along with Charles Lyell and William Buckland, had brazenly postulated that the diluvial phenomena previously attributed to the Noahic flood, had, theoretically, been caused by the huge, extinct ice sheets. The Ice Age, therefore, replaced the flood as the primary causative agent responsible for shaping the earth's surface. As Enlightenment "scientists," they resolutely rejected the revelation of God through Scripture and froze out the flood. They simply turned water to ice and then applied the naturalistic, uniformitarian principles of Lyell to the process so as to gain credibility for an "old" earth concept.

What met with resistance from the pulpits was greeted with enthusiasm in the great universities of Europe and in some of the increasingly secularized institutions of the United States. When Charles Darwin later postulated his theory of biological evolution, (*The Origin of Species,* 1859) he simply built on the dual foundations of uniformitarianism, laid down by Charles Lyell (*Principles of Geology,* 1830), and the glacial theory of Agassiz. The protests and refutations did not stop, as we well know, but evolution became entrenched in a widening bed of academic receptivity which preferred fanciful fables to the authority of God's Word.

Glacial theory must be exposed for the hoax that it is because it is neither scientific nor sensible. It was designed to advance uniformitarian principles, which are essential to the practice of naturalistic science, but it flaunts the very principles it claims to espouse. Uniformitarianism is the widely held assumption that the past history of the earth was wholly uniform and stable in its naturalistic processes, thereby allowing naturalists to extrapolate backwards in time from present events and processes. By allegiance to this unbiblical presupposition, scientists then and now attempt to explain natural history without recourse to any supernatural explanations, miracles, or catastrophes. Uniformitarians found it unacceptable to invoke one-time catastrophic occurrences such as the flood as explanation for all the geological phenomena around us. They chose instead to deny God and to attribute all the phenomena to natural processes which occurred at a uniform rate and pattern throughout history. If a glacier moved at a rate of five foot per year, it would take sixteen million years for one to move from the North Pole to the Ohio River and then for it to recede the same distance. The theory *assumes* that such actually happened, but the theory fails to consider the very non-uniform patterns that would have had to occur in order for such an event to happen.

The earth would have had to tilt radically on its axis in order for a glacier of that magnitude to form and then reach below the Mason-Dixon line. Simultaneously, the earth's rotation would have had to stop in order for glaciers to cover Europe and Asia as well as the U.S. and Canada. What could possibly have caused such potentially catastrophic shiftings of the earth in its orbit? What was happening in the Southern Hemisphere while the Northern was being put into a freezer? Did the Southern Hemisphere, including Antartica, boil and bake for eons while the North froze?

To argue that glaciers scooped out the thousands of lakes in Michigan, Wisconsin, and Minnesota seems to have some plausibility until one starts to think about the host of inconsistencies involved in such a conjecture. Why would glaciers, operating from uniformitarian principles, leave gently rolling hills everywhere in their path? Why not the effects of mindless bulldozers, leveling everything on their routes? Why are there deep troughs and trenches on the floors of the Great Lakes, some running east to west, while others crisscross in north to south patterns? How could these glaciers "create" the Niagara escarpment, with its south to north drop-off, when the theory dictates that the drop-off should have been from north to south? Why does the theory locate the glaciers in the warm, lower elevations of the midwestern states when it would have been much more scientifically plausible to have positioned them in the upper, colder elevations of the mountain states?

In some versions of the Glacial Epoch theory, the mythology takes on even stranger fantasies. In the printed materials of Chicago's Museum of Natural

History, it is hypothesized that most of Illinois and Kentucky were once lush equatorial swamps surrounded by the saline Sea of Illinois. After these primeval rain forests sank beneath the surface of the earth, the climate changed drastically and the Great Ice Age followed on its heels. Such widely divergent fantasies may be "scientific" explanations for both the deposits of coal and of fossils, but they require even more catastrophic shifts in the earth's orbit than does the Glacial Epoch theory when it is offered in simpler, isolated form.

To call into question what has become almost universally accepted usually does not create an immediate circle of friends. Prior to drafting this article, I broached the subject of glaciers with both friends and relatives, most of whom were professing Christians. I was surprised and disappointed at how deeply the Glacial Epoch theory had become embedded in their belief patterns. Of course this land was once covered with glaciers, they said, for the notion was never questioned when it appeared in their and their children's textbooks. It is molded into tablets of iron and stone in numerous state parks and emblazoned on the plaques of the National Park Service. The majority of "scientists" believe it, and they would never prevaricate the truth. I have even heard it proclaimed from our pulpits. So it goes.

No matter what the political consequences, we owe it to ourselves and our students to know the truth. We have made a promise to God that we would teach His children the truth, the whole truth, and nothing but the truth. When we do that, we will be accused of ignorance, of naivete, and of antiscientific attitudes. Some of us may shrink under such attacks, but if we are seeing reality through the spectacles of God's Word, we are standing on the rock that cannot be shaken.

To subject the Glacial Epoch theory to scrutiny is simply to practice good science, for "science" has always been defined as "knowledge." It was the pseudoscience of Charles Lyell and Louis Agassiz that undermined the Noahic flood. It is belief in their theories and commitment to their "proof" (selected evidence submitted on behalf of an hypothesis) that has eroded our faith in the first eleven chapters of Genesis.

Some weeks ago Howard Van Til (*The Fourth Day*) passionately pleaded with me never to tell my students or my readers that there was a Noahic flood. There is simply no "scientific" evidence for such, he argued. I made a promise in reply. As long as I am a child of God, I will believe Him and His Word, where He says it was *water*. Louis Agassiz's disciples may claim that it was *ice,* but their ill-devised myths are sorely lacking in credibility. When it comes to a choice between ice or water, I will stick with water.

Appendix B
Replies to a Geologist

THE preceding chapter was originally published as an article in *Christian Renewal*. It precipitated a number of letters, both favorable and condemnatory. Apparently it touched a raw nerve among evolutionists. One geologist in particular thought it worthy of a series of rebuttals. That correspondence is illuminating.

27 June 1988

Dr. Norman De Jong
Trinity Christian College
6601 W. College Dr.
Palos Heights, IL 60463

Dear Norm:

I recently returned to Grand Rapids and the Calvin campus at the conclusion of a study leave. In the process of doing some catching up on my reading, I read your article "Ice or Water?" in the March 21, 1988, issue of *Christian Renewal*.

I am more than a little surprised that you would write such an article before you had done a more thorough study of the topic at hand. There are detailed presentations of the glacial explanations of the landforms of the upper Midwest and other parts of the continents of the Northern Hemisphere in many geology textbooks. Many of those textbooks present a detailed description of the evidence on which the glacial explanation is based. One of the books which I recommend that you place on your personal bookshelf is *Geology Illustrated* by John S. Shelton, published by Freeman. I am enclosing photocopies of Chapters 18 and 31 of that book for your information. Photocopies of the photographs are not nearly as good as the photographs themselves, so I recommend that you get a copy of the book. I also heartily recommend that you take a list of evidences for glaciation in hand, and go out and look at those landforms with your own eyes. Examine them in detail to see for yourself whether the claims made in the textbooks are true.

I am also enclosing a copy of a letter which I have sent to *Christian Renewal* with the request that it be printed in the "Readers' Viewpoint" column of that publication.

If you would like to pursue the study of geology in more detail, I would be pleased to recommend study materials and to help you in your study in any way that I can.

Sincerely,

Clarence Menninga
Professor of Geology

*   *   *

27 June 1988

Mr. John Hultink, Editor
Christian Renewal
P.O. Box 770
Lewiston, NY 14092

Dear Mr. Hultink:

Please place the following comments in the "Readers' Viewpoint" column of *CR* at the earliest opportunity.

Dear readers of *Christian Renewal*:

In the March 21, 1988, issue of *CR* (pp. 10–11), Dr. Norman De Jong suggests that the surface deposits and landforms in Wisconsin, Michigan, and other northern regions of continents in the Northern Hemisphere are not the result of glaciation, as is usually taught and argued, but that those deposits are the result of the Flood described in Genesis.

Dr. De Jong suggests that the glacial explanation of those deposits has been accepted merely because it has been taught in secular universities, proclaimed in secular museum displays, and inserted into school textbooks. However, many of us have accepted the glacial explanation

APPENDIX B 73

of those deposits because of persuasive evidence, and not just because we have mindlessly accepted what Dr. De Jong calls "ill-devised myths." I recommend that you get the book *Geology Illustrated* (written by John S. Shelton) from your local public or college library and read about that evidence (Chapters 18 and 31). If you have opportunity to do so, go and look at those deposits and examine the evidence for yourself.

Dr. De Jong correctly identifies Louis Agassiz as the first author and proponent of that glacial explanation. Dr. De Jong presents the work of Agassiz as if it proceeded from a philosophy of godless naturalism, antagonistic to God and to the Bible. That picture of Agassiz as a godless opponent of Christianity is completely false. Agassiz was a devout Christian for his entire life. Agassiz firmly believed (as I do) that the design and orderliness which we see in the universe shows the handiwork of the Divine Designer. However, Agassiz did not consider his glacial explanation of surface deposits to be a contradiction to Scripture. In his geological study of glaciers and glacial deposits, Agassiz was faithfully applying his Christian conception of God as orderly Designer to his study of God's world.

There are some serious questions which we should be discussing about the theological meaning of the Flood described in Genesis and about how the results of geological study fit with the Scriptures. But rejecting the glacial explanation of those surface deposits is not the correct answer to those theological questions.

Clarence Menninga
Grand Rapids, Michigan

*　　　*　　　*

July 11, 1988

John Van Dyk
Christian Renewal
P.O. Box 770
Lewiston, NY 14092

Dear John:

I recently received a copy of a letter from Clarence Menninga, which he wishes you to publish in response to my "Ice or Water" article in your Mar. 21 issue. Since the topic is of such significance to the Reformed community, I have drafted a reply to his letter. It is long, I know, but the debate is complex and the issues are far from resolved. With your permission, I would like to have my reply printed in the same issue as his letter.

Cordially,
Norman De Jong

*   *   *

Dear Clarence:

I want to thank you for the courtesy of sending me an advance copy of the letter which you addressed to *Christian Renewal*, thereby giving me opportunity to respond. If you don't mind, I would like to reply to your various thoughts in reverse order, starting with your last paragraph and proceeding to the more technical concepts you suggest in paragraph two.

You say that "there are some serious questions which we should be discussing about the theological meaning of the Flood described in Genesis." What are these "serious questions" that you have? You don't say, but only leave us guessing! You suggest that there are *theological* problems, but don't identify those either. Do you think a Flood ever occurred, or do you insist, along with Howard Van Til, that there is "no scientific evidence" for a Flood?

You come to the defense of Louis Agassiz and claim that he "was a devout Christian for his entire life." Jimmy Swaggart makes the same profession. So did Thomas Jefferson. Does that make any one of them worthy of devotion and blind adherence to their teaching? If Agassiz was a Christian, I would have to conclude that he was certainly not Calvinistic in his interpretations and was obviously not guided by Scripture in his thinking. His life-long insistence that we should "study nature, not books" is a classic example of Enlightenment thought which rejected special revelation and the divine authorship of Scripture. It is interesting to note, too, that he violated his own dictum by writing a number of books which he expected his own disciples to blindly believe as gospel truth. It seems, from your comments, that you are one of those adherents.

I appreciate receiving from you photocopies of Chapters 18 and 31 of *Geology Illustrated* by John S. Shelton. Be assured that I have read them carefully, as you suggested. I assume, from your references, that this is a book which you require your students to read at Calvin.

There are a number of reactions to these chapters which I would like to share with you, not all of which can be contained in this letter, which certainly will become too long.

First of all, Shelton very pointedly reinforces all of the major points which I tried to make in my article on *Ice or Water*. Concerning the antithetical relationship between the flood account of Genesis and the Ice Age theory, Shelton says:

> "Geology was not a science until the legendary flood and six-day creation were replaced by explanations derived from careful study of rocks. The doctrine that past events should be explainable through no more than reasonable extensions of observable processes has played a vital role in substituting the plausible for the preposterous and the feasible for the fanciful in geology" (p. 351).

Shelton thereby reduces all the Biblical accounts of and references (not limited incidentally to Gen. 6-8) to the Flood as "legendary," "preposterous," and "fanciful." For Shelton and Agassiz it was not a both/and, but an either/or proposition.

A second concern of mine is that you nowhere suggest that this material from Shelton should be studied with a critical, discerning eye. You recommend the book without stating any reservations. That scares me because the typical college student, who does not yet know how to be astutely critical, will glibly swallow this nonsense because he is by nature a believer. He needs and wants to believe.

Your job as professor is not to treat him like a sponge, but to develop his critical, discerning skills so that he may learn to "test the spirits to see whether they are from God, because many false prophets have gone out into the world" (I John 4:1). You and I need to warn our students constantly that there are "false prophets among the people, just as there will be false teachers among you" (II Peter 2:1). We need daily to put on the spectacles of Scripture and to "reject with all our hearts whatsoever does not agree with this infallible rule" (Belg. Conf., Art. VII).

You and I, who would be teachers, need to be reminded by our Lord and King that whoever leads one of these chosen ones astray, "it would be better for him to be thrown into the sea with a millstone tied around his neck than for him to cause one of these little ones to sin" (Lk. 17:2).

Thirdly, the gist of Chapters 18 and 31 is that everything must be explained in terms of naturalistic, evolutionary processes. There is no room whatsoever for divine involvement. These two chapters are naturalistic evolution at its worst. Shelton makes no bones about the fact that he is trying to amass evidence which will support his hypothesis of an Ice Age Epoch. Page after page reads like an obsession with finding some kind, any kind, of evidence to prove or substantiate his belief in glacial epochs already held because of religious and a priori commitments. Shelton is not a neutral, objective scientist and never pretends to be. He is an unabashed, proud salesman of Agassiz's ideas.

We must remember, of course, that there never have been and never will be neutral, objective scientists. Shelton's prior commitment to evolutionary ice age theory dictates what kind of evidence he will look for, what he will accept when he sees it, and what counter-evidence he will blissfully ignore because it conflicts with the theory he is trying to prove. Proof, you know, is nothing more than evidence presented on behalf of a belief. Our beliefs, in turn, are controlled by unspoken assumptions and presuppositions, such as your commitment to uniformitarianism. Your core belief in the uniformity of all natural processes dictates for you and all other self-proclaimed "scientists" how you conduct your "scientific" inquiry. Shelton, for example, confuses and interchanges volcanic activity and glacial activity as though they are one and the same. Whenever he can't explain something that is too big to ignore, he simply labels it as an "erratic" and then turns his back on it. He frequently has a mysterious, almost amusing way of shifting from "probable" and "possible" explanations on one page to "the only possible" explanation on the next. He violates the law of the excluded middle so often that it would make a logician's head spin. Shelton's book is not only an illustration of horrendous logic, but bad science besides. As such, it could become an effective tool for teaching discernment skills to your students.

The last section of Chap. 31 is entitled *Pleistocene Lakes of the Great Basin* (pp. 352-363). In it Shelton is trying to muster evidence for his belief that the last great Ice Age covered North America approximately 10,000 to 12,000 years before Christ. He deals primarily with "evidence" from the large intermountain basin that covers much of Utah, Nevada, and central California down to the Mexican border. He argues that the Great Salt Lake, Death Valley, the Salton Sea, and everything in between were formed by this last great glacier, yet all of the "evidence" that Shelton submits would make much greater "scientific" sense if it were attributed to a massive flood. Shelton, however, has relegated any arguments for a flood to the categories of legendary, preposterous, and fanciful.

Consider, for example, some of these quotations from your trusted authority:

> "Every Great Basin depression that has been studied in detail gives evidence of having been filled with water" (p. 362)

> "The fact that shoreline features are rather well preserved throughout the Great Basin, even when developed on loose sand

and gravel, has led all who have studied them to conclude that they are geologically quite recent. But the likely hypothesis that they are in some way connected with the Pleistocene Ice Age is more difficult to prove and refine than one might think" (p. 360).

"Even in today's most arid part of the Great Basin, there is widespread evidence not only of former lakes, but also of connecting rivers. The view of the Arrow Canyon in southern Nevada shows part of one of the many gorges cut by such rivers in the southern part of the Great Basin. Only a powerful stream working rather rapidly could produce such steep walls, yet these canyons are now either dry or contain only an intermittent trickle" (p. 356).

"The last advance of the Pleistocene Ice sheet . . . pushed over trees whose Carbon content places the event at about 11,800 years ago . . . this conclusion is independent of whether or not C gives *true* age values; it requires only that they be consistent" (p. 362).

If you are a priori committed to a glacial epoch theory, these chapters from Shelton might seem appealing and might even reinforce your presuppositions. If you do not hold to such a theory, but approach them with critical examination, the argument that Shelton advances is as porous as sand.

In conclusion, let me thank you again for sending the chapters from Shelton. They reinforced my commitment to the infallibility of the Scriptures and strengthened my conviction that a great Noahic flood makes much more "scientific" sense than does any glacial epoch theory.

Cordially yours,
Norman De Jong

*   *   *

17 September 1988

Dr. Norman De Jong
Trinity Christian College
6601 W. College Dr.
Palos Heights, IL 60463

Dear Norm:

I have noticed that my letter to *Christian Renewal* about "Ice or Water" was published in the most recent issue, along with your response.

If you come to Grand Rapids sometime, and you have a few hours of time to spare, and if my schedule permits, I would like to take you to a few places in the Grand Rapids area to see some rocks and some landforms. What we say about God's world ought to fit with what we see in God's world.

Sincerely yours,
In Christ,

Clarence Menninga
Professor of Geology

*   *   *

6 November 1988

Dr. Norman De Jong
Trinity Christian College
6601 W. College Dr.
Palos Heights, IL 60463

Dear Norm:

After my last letter to you (17 September 1988), I had not intended to write to you again until you had accepted my invitation to guide you on a geology field trip. Even after the forum in which you participated on 27 October in Calvin's FAA, I would not likely have written. But, obviously, here I am, writing again.

I changed my mind about not writing because of a conversation I had a couple of weeks ago with Marvin and Helen Van Wyck. My wife and I had gone to express our condolences to the Hoekema family after Tony had died. I have known Marv since he was a student in a couple of my classes, and we talked for quite a while, much of that time about you. Marv testified that you are a very caring, Christian man. He told me of your comforting visit with them after Helen's father died. He assured me that you are very sincere in your efforts to understand God's Word properly, and that you are very eager to serve God in your teaching and living and in your influence on students and other fellow Christians. On the basis of that testimony, I will assume that your sincerity extends to your efforts to learn about God's world so that you can understand it properly, also. And on that basis, I am writing to you to make a few additional comments about God's world.

First, I have a few questions:

1. Have you ever visited an active glacier? Have you seen with your own two eyes the mass of ice called a glacier? Have you seen with your own two eyes the circumstances in which glaciers exist? Have you seen with your own two eyes the sorts of deposits and landforms which are found with glaciers and which were produced by the action of those glaciers?

2. Where did you get the idea that the entire Rocky Mountain Range was covered with a solid sheet of glacier ice during the time that we call the Ice Age?

3. Where did you get the idea that the Great Basin was covered with glacier ice during the time that we call the Ice Age?

The questions about glaciers which you asked at the forum on 27 October 1988 do have answers. The questions have been investigated thoroughly, and the answers to those questions have been well verified, and they make good sense. The conclusions are not at all preposterous.

I cannot give you a lot of detail in the answers to those questions within the space of a letter, so the following comments are just the barest minimum of information to indicate what those answers are. More details are readily available, however, in books. I would even be willing to elaborate on any of those answers, if you wish, in response to questions which you still have.

Glacier ice forms wherever there is a greater amount of annual snow fall than annual snow melt. The net accumulation of water in its solid state produces an annual increase in the thickness of the ice at that location until the weight of the overlying ice produces a flow of ice to a lower elevation. In the locations where there are glaciers today, the long term average flow of ice is nearly the same as the long term average accumulation of ice, so that the accumulation and flow are in equilibrium. At lower elevation and higher temperatures, the ice melts at the "toe" or "snout" or "edge" of the glacier. The melt rate at the toe of the glacier is in equilibrium with the flow rate of glacier ice from higher elevation.

At the present time, there is a net accumulation of snow at the higher elevations in many mountains and mountain ranges. These "Alpine" glaciers, or "mountain" glaciers, flow down the valleys of those mountains to lower elevations, where the ice melts. Rocks of various sizes and rock rubble are formed by weathering of the exposed bedrock in and along the sides of those valleys, and those rocks and rock rubble are carried down along with the ice. Those rocks and rock rubble are left at the melting snout and sides of the glacier ice at lower elevations. These piles of rock and rock rubble form the moraines which are characteristic of transportation of sediments by ice.

Where glacier ice extends out to the shoreline of the ocean from the mountain range or from the continental ice mass, the ice breaks off from the glacier in huge chunks call "icebergs." The rocks and rock rubble which are carried with the icebergs are dropped to the ocean floor when that ice melts. The ocean floor off the coasts of Greenland and Antarctica is littered with such rocks.

The ice of glaciers is formed from snow which fell on that region. The snow is formed from water which has been evaporated from the world's oceans. That is where the water comes from to form the glaciers which exist today. That is where the water came from to form the masses of continental glaciers which covered parts of North America, Europe, and Asia during the Ice Age, too. During the time that the greatest amount of ice existed on those land masses, sea level was about 300 feet lower than it is today. Sea level was lower because that much water had been withdrawn from the oceans and was temporarily stored in those masses of ice. That amount of water is adequate to produce the amount of ice present in those continental glaciers. There is a lot of evidence which supports the conclusion that sea level was 300 feet below present levels during that time. This evidence is independent of the evidence for the presence of glaciers in North Central and Northeastern United States during that time.

These two lines of evidence—glacial deposits and lower sea level—plus evidence for a cooler worldwide climate during the Ice Age, fit with the conclusion that such glaciation did occur. The evidence is not consistent with the proposal that the surface deposits of the Upper Midwest of the United States are the result of a worldwide flood. That does NOT say that such a flood did not occur; it DOES say that the surface deposits found in much of Wisconsin, Michigan, and most of Illinois are not the product of flood waters, but are the product of transport and deposition of sediments by glacial ice.

What we say about God's world should fit with what we see in God's world.

Norm, I am sending copies of this letter to several people in addition to yourself. It is my opinion that you are no longer entitled to be protected from public embarrassment by the privacy of personal correspondence when you make public pronouncements about matters to which you have given little serious study. It is evident from your comments in the forum on 27 October 1988 that you had made little or no attempt to read and understand the materials on glaciers which I had sent to you earlier. At the same time, I am willing to help you to greater knowledge and under-standing, if you are, as Marv Van Wyck testifies, sincere in your desire to know and publish the truth about God's world and God's Word.

                              Sincerely yours,
                              In Christ,

                              Clarence Menninga

              *   *   *

                              November 14, 1988

Dr. Clarence Menninga
Dept. of Geology
Calvin College
Grand Rapids, MI 49506

Dear Clarence:

Thank you for taking the time to write the lengthy, fascinating letter of November 6. In contrast to your terse letter of September 17, you express much more openness toward dialogue and meaningful exchange of ideas than you did at that time, so I judge now that an equally lengthy reply would be in order.

Your supportive comments about my response to the death of Tony Hoekema and to the sorrow of the Van Wycks are deeply appreciated, even though I find it difficult to fathom why they found their way into a letter whose stated purpose is to cause me public embarrassment. Marv and Helen were equally puzzled and would much prefer not to be drawn into our disagreements on these scientific issues. I trust that no further reference to their sadness need be made.

I chose not to respond to your September 17 letter because I see little or no profit in looking at "some rocks and some landforms in the Grand Rapids area." It was obvious from that letter, which can hardly be construed as an answer to the array of issues I raised in our exchange on the pages of the Sept. 12, 1988 issue of *Christian Renewal*, that you wanted to take me on a walking tour of some quarries or river beds. You want me to spend part of a day looking at some striated rocks and thereby to conclude that Louis Agassiz's theory of glacial epochs is the truth. I would much prefer to spend that time in the quiet of my study reading some passages from the Words of God. Agassiz and all of his cub reporters only have a few time-worn shards of shrapnel for evidence. God was not only there, but He caused it all to happen, directed its conclusion, and reported live from the scene.

Let me illustrate by way of analogy. This past October we once again enjoyed and/or endured the World Series. I could not be there because of distance, cost, and a few other factors. It was quite an event, especially because of Orel Hershiser's public praise to God after each of his masterful accomplishments. I had at least two options relative to the Series. I could read about it in the newspapers the next day and get an inning by inning account of each game by live reporters on the scene. That route, I suspect, was pretty accurate, sufficiently vivid, and thoroughly satisfying, even though numerous details were missing, and I was not there in person to satiate every idle curiosity.

The second option would be to wait for the "scientists" to arrive on the scene and to examine the evidence. After writing and polishing numerous grant proposals to the various governments agencies, they would eventually receive funding to travel to both Oakland and L.A. to "examine the evidence." Once there, they could ferret out "the evidence" in the form of scratched baseballs, stretched gloves, bruised bats, dented fences, and torn program fragments. From these and sundry other sources, they could "scientifically" stitch together what occurred in that monumental and emotional warfare called the Series.

But you probably object. How improbable that they would ever be able, long after the event occurred, to fashion an account that bore any semblance to reality! Why not trust the authors who were there?

You get the point, I trust. When all the nineteenth and twentieth century scientists, yourself included, persist in rejecting the Biblical account of the Noahic flood, they and you are slapping the face and claiming superiority over the omniscient Author who was on the scene. You come up instead with some fanciful and scientifically untenable stories about glacial epochs and ice-age theories.

But let me return to your invitation "to come to Grand Rapids to see some rocks." In comparison to other experiences in my life, I did not think that a Grand Rapids trip would compare very favorably.

In answer to your first question, "have you ever seen with your own two eyes?" the answer is an emphatic *yes!* You should remember from my very first article in the *Christian Renewal* that I never came close to denying the existence of glaciers. We lived for three years in Montana and could look at the glaciers in the Spanish Peaks any day we wanted. We also camped for a week in Glacier National Park and studied the literature carefully. The bulk of your second page, therefore, is quite agreeable to me and beyond the scope of our disagreements.

What I object to is your assertion that great parts of North America, Europe, and Asia, were "covered by glaciers during the Ice Age." That is what I find to be absolutely preposterous and contrary to all the uniformitarian principles with which many natural scientists insist on working.

To argue from the existence of glaciers to the existence of an ice-age is illogical and unwarranted. It would be equally invalid to argue from the existence of a flood in Michigan to the existence of the Noahic flood. We simply should not start with empirical evidence and from that try to prove or disprove the biblical account. What we as Calvinists, who agree with Article VII of the Belgic Confession, should be doing is starting with the infallible, divinely-authored Scriptures as truth. Given the plain teaching of God's Word concerning His anger at sin, and given the details of Genesis 6,7, and 8, we can accept the account of the Noahic flood as truth. Then, when we see floods around our own communities, we can see the tremendous power of water and the devastation that it can wreak in a very short time.

We moved to Montana in 1960, shortly after the massive earthquakes in Yellowstone Park and the ensuing floods in the Madison River Valley. The consequences and damages from both sides of that cataclysmic event were awesome. In 1972 we traveled through the Black Hills after a major flood occurred there. In 1976 we were in Rocky Mountain National Park during the flood that devastated Thompson Canyon. Over the years we have traveled extensively throughout the Rocky Mountains of both the U.S. and Western Canada, have toured such places as Hell's Gate, Montana, the Lewis and Clark Caverns, and Mammoth Caves in Kentucky. We have visited the Niagara Escarpment on numerous occasions and many other interesting places. We have seen many fascinating geological formations and have looked at a number of fossils in a variety of museums. At no time have I seen any convincing evidence that any of these phenomena were caused by glaciers. There is extensive evidence, however, that many of these could have been caused by the kind of flood and the accompanying earthquakes that are described in Genesis. The Noahic flood would also be a much more plausible explanation for the apparently lower sea levels (about 300 feet) that you describe in your letter. The continental shelf is a fascinating phenomena, as are the ocean trenches that reach depths equal to the height of the Himalayas. None of those can be explained by glaciers, no matter how you contort the theory.

You ask where I get the idea that the Great Basin was covered with ice during the Ice Age? The answer is from multiple sources. In the *Christian Renewal* of Sept. 12, 1988 I quoted extensively from the book *Geology Illustrated* by John Shelton, which you sent me. I dealt with that book in a careful critical analysis, but your letter of September 17 gave the impression that you had not even read my analysis. In addition to that source I have visited the Museum of Natural History in Chicago, which devotes at least one sixth of its viewing space to propaganda for Louis Agassiz's theory. My assessment of their display would be comparable to that of Shelton's book.

I trust that these reactions will be carefully analyzed before you once again invite me to come to Grand Rapids and "look at some land forms." When I get there I have so many relatives and friends to visit and so little time to see them that they would be upset if I spent that time trekking through stream beds or quarries looking for evidence of glacial epochs. Sorry about that choice of priorities.

All the folks to whom you sent your letter are probably hoping that they will not get on any more mailing lists, but I'll send copies to those who have not pointedly asked to be removed. They can read it or toss it in the circular file.

Cordially yours,

Norman De Jong

NDJ/ss

For Further Discussion

1. The book by John Shelton claims that at one time Death Valley was a lake at least 600 feet deep and more than 100 miles long (p. 358). He also argues that Lake Bonneville, just north of Salt Lake City, at one time was at least 1000 feet above the present lake (p. 355). If these figures are credible, how would you explain them?

    a. do glaciers ever melt so fast as to cause such massive run-off?
    b. what could possibly have caused such melting?
    c. if such dry lake beds are truly found on the western side of the Continental Divide, why would we not find similar glacial run-off basins on the east side?

2. Since you and numerous geology texts claim that the land forms in the northern half of the northern hemisphere were covered with and formed by continental glaciers, how do you then explain similar land forms in Central America, South America, the Hawaiian Islands, Tibet, Malaysia, and Kenya? Were they also formed by glaciers? Was the entire planet a big ice ball sometime after the "Big Bang"?

3. Since ice is understood to be frozen water, where did all the water come from that formed your glaciers? How did it manage to get so deep and widespread as to cover half of North America, most of Europe, and most of Asia? And why did it freeze? Was the earth tilted on its axis away from the sun for millions of years? If so, what happens to the uniformitarian principles of Charles Lyell?

4. If you insist on explaining mountains, canyons, and lakes as a result of glaciation, how do you explain the deep valleys and trenches in the ocean floor? Were they also carved by glaciers?

CHAPTER SIX

Appendix C
Organizations Formed to
React to Evolutionism

THIS first organization was formed to combat the effects of evolutionism and differs from those listed below in the diversity of views of creation held by its members.

American Scientific Affiliation (1941)
Box J
Ipswich, MA 01938

The following organizations hold specificially to a young earth interpretation of Genesis account of creation or have a substantial membership which does.

Creation Research Society (1963)
2717 Cranbrook Road
Ann Arbor, MI 48104

Creation Science Association of Ontario
P.O. Box 821, Station A
Scarborough, Ontario M1K 5C8

Creation Science Reasearch Center (1970)
P.O. Box 23195
San Diego, CA 92123

Institute for Creation Research (1972)
2100 Greenfield Dr.
El Cajon, CA 92021

Students for Origins Research (1977)

P.O. Box 203
Goleta, CA 93116

Creation, Social Science and Humanities Society (1977)
1429 N. Holyoke
Wichita, KA 67208

Bible-Science Association
2911 E. 42nd Street
Minneapolis, MN 55408

The Creation Concerns, Inc.
Portland, OR

Origins Geoscience Research Institute
Loma Linda University
Loma Linda, CA 92350

Missouri Association for Creation
P.O. Box 23984
St. Louis, MO 63119

Center for Scientific Creation (1982)
1314 Brush Hill Circle
Naperville, IL 60540

Fellowshop of Saved Scientists and Interested Laymen (1983)
77 Parker Street
Jamestown, NY 14701

Creation Science Foundation (1983)
(Publishes the magazine, EX NIHILO)
P.O. Box 6064
Evanston, IL 60204

Organizations focusing on publishing filmstrips and courses are:

Creation Filmstrip Center
Route 1
Haviland, KA 67059

George Fox College (A recent videotape course—"Creation Science: A New Perspective on Origins".)
Newberg, OR 97132

Some organizations which have come out strongly against creationists:

Committees on Correspondence (1980)
156 East Altat Vista
Ottumwa, IA 52501

"The Committees on Correspondence are a nationwide communications network committed to the defense of education in evolutionary theory." They have organizations in most states at present. They function to "reprint news items of evolutionist and creationist activities, suggest tactics, legislative and judicial developments, and the like."

Creation/Evolution Journal
P.O. Box 5
Amherst Branch
Buffalo, NY 14226

"This is the only publication of its kind, one devoted exclusively to the raging controversy over creationism in the public schools. In its pages are the well-researched scientific answers to creationists arguments. Included also are the practical responses to creationist legal and educational actions." (Taken from their advertisement)

American Association for the Advancement of Science
1515 Massechusetts Ave. NW
Washington, D.C. 20005

They have published several articles each year since 1980 critical of the creationists in *Science* and in the December 1981 issue of *Science 81* had a pull-out section designed to combat creationism. This section was made available to all high school teachers in the United States.

National Association of Biology Teachers
11250 Roger Bacon Drive #19
Reston, VA 22090

American Institute of Biological Sciences (Publishers of Bioscience)
1401 Wilson Blvd
Arlington, VA 22209

American Civil Liberties Union

Recent books designed to refute creationst claims and present, in nontechnical terms, the case for evolution:

Ruse, Michael, 1982. *Darwinism Defended: A Guide to the Evolutionary Controversies,* Addison-Wesley Publishing Co., Reading, Mass.

Futuyma, Douglas, 1983. *Science on Trial: A Case for Evolution,* Pantheon Books, Dept 15-25C, 201 East 50th St., NY. NY. 10022

Kitcher, Philip, 1982. *Abusing Science: A Case Against Creation,* The MIT Press, Cambridge, Mass. 213 pp.

Montagu, Ashley, Editor, 1984. *Science and Creationism,* Oxford University Press, New York, N.Y., 415 pp.

Notes

1. National Academy of Sciences, *Science and Creationism,* (Washington, D.C., 1984), pp. 5–6.

2. Rom. 12:2 (NIV).

3. *Science and Creationism,* p.6.

4. Howard Van Til, *The Fourth Day,* (Grand Rapids, Mich.: Wm. B. Eerdmans Pub. Co., 1986), p. 267.

5. The Confession of Faith, Article II. Also and usually known as the Belgic Confession because it originated in Belgium. It was adopted by the great Synod of Dort in 1618–19 as one of the Doctrinal Standards of the Reformed Churches. The complete text is available from almost any Reformed denomination.

6. Howard Van Til; Davis Young; and Clarence Menninga, *Science Held Hostage,* (Downers Grove: Intervarsity Press. 1988), 189 pages.

7. Ibid., p.10.

8. Ibid., p.29.

9. Stephen Jay Gould, "Knight Takes Bishop? The facts about the Great Wilberforce-Huxley Debate Don't Always Fit the Legend," *Natural History,* May 1986, p.20.

10. Ibid., p.32.

11. Hodge, *What is Darwinism?* p.126.

12. Ibid., p.142.

13. Andrew Dickson White, *A History of the Warfare of Science with Theology,* Vol.1, (New York: Dover Publications, Inc,, 1896), p.viii. It should be noted that two pages later he reverts to a stance of feigned neutrality, claiming to "present a clear and impartial statement of the views and acts of the two contending parties. I have endeavored to stand aloof, and relate with impartiality their actions." (p.ix)

14. Draper, *History of the Conflict,* p.vi.

15. Ibid., p.xi.

16. Ibid.

17. Gould, "Knight Takes Bishop?" p.32.

18. Ibid.

19. Ibid.

20. Lindberg and Numbers, "Beyond War and Peace," p.3.

21. Ibid., p.3.

22. Ibid., p.12.

23. Charles Hodge, *What Is Darwinism?*, p. 126.

24. Charles Lyell, *Principles of Geology*, Vol. I, p. 164.

25. Gould, *American Scientist*, Vol. 74, p. 61.

26. Eric Hoffer, *The True Believer*, p. 18.

27. For insight into what I think is a corrected version of early American religious history, see *Separation of Church and State: The Myth Revisited*, Paideia Press, coauthored with Jack Van Der Slik, pp. xiii–xix.

28. N. Wolterstorff, *Curriculum: By What Standard* (Grand Rapids: National Union of Christian Schools, 1966), p. 2.

29. Howard Van Til, *The Fourth Day*, p. 209

30. Ibid.

31. For a sampling of the various reactions to it, consult "How It All Began," *Christianity Today*, August 12, 1988, pp. 31–34.

32. *The Fourth Day*, p. 246

33. For a detailed description of this well known educational conflict, see H.G. Good, *A History of American Education*, Second Edition (New York: The Macmillan Col, 1962), pp. 161–6.

34. Westminster Confession, Chap. IV. I

35. Confession of Faith, Art. XII, par. 1

36. All passages are taken from the NIV. The terminology is even more difficult to interpret in some other versions.

37. See Luke 3:36. This represents a minor problem of textual criticisms, not adequately explained. Some scholars use this example to attack the authenticity or infallibility of Scripture, but it need not concern us here.

38. It should be noted that the New Testament begins with a genealogy of Christ (Matt. 1:1–17). It is not included here because that one ignores the line from Adam to Abraham. Matthew begins with Abraham because he was writing to a Jewish audience.

39. For an excellent treatment of this subject, see Kenneth A. Ham. *The Lie: Evolution*. (Creation-Life Publishers, El Cajon, CA), 1987

40. Howard Van Til, *The Fourth Day*, pp. 180 and 236.

41. Ibid., p. 270.

42. Ibid., p. 237. For a detailed examination of this argument from the evolutionists' perspective, read pp. 236–242.

43. Ibid., p. 240.

44. See our discussion of *uniformitarianism* in Chapter 4 and the Appendices.

45. Alan Dundes, ed., *The Flood Myth*, p.3.

46. Matt. 24:36. See also Acts 1:7.

47. Based on the Biblical evidence, we have concluded that the earth is "young," certainly not less than six thousand years old, and probably not

much more than that. We need to be open to the possibility that the seven "days" of creation were more than twenty-four hour periods and also that there is a significant time-gap between Gen. 1:1 and 2.

48. Job 1:1 and 3b.
49. Job 38:2–3.
50. Job 42:2–3.
51. John S. Shelton, *Geology Illustrated* (San Francisco: W. H. Freeman & Co., 1966). The reader will recall that this is the book recommended so highly by Clarence Menninga and critiqued in the preceding chapters.
52. Gen. 7:11 (NIV)
53. Gen. 9:15
54. Isaiah 54: 5 & 9
55. Gen. 9:16

Bibliography

Aardsma, Gerald E. "Myths Regarding Radiocarbon Dating." *Impact,* (Institute for Creation Research) 189 (March 1989).

Adams, Charles. "Making Technology a Signpost of the Kingdom." *Dordt College Voice* 32 no. 1 (October, 1986).

Agassiz, Louis. *Methods of Study in Natural History,* New York: Arno Press, 1970, 1863, 319 pp.

Agassiz, Louis. *Principles of Zoology.* New York: Arno Press, 1970, 1848, 216 pp.

Agassiz, Louis. *Studies on Glaciers.* Carozzi, Albert Translator and ed., Hafner, 1967.

Ashworth, William B. "Catholicism and Early Modern Science." *God and Nature.* Lindberg and Numbers, eds. Berkeley: University of California Press, 1986, pp. 136–166.

Bennetta, Wm. J., ed. *Crusade of the Credulous.* San Fransisco, Ca.: California Academy of Sciences, 1986, 36 pp.

Bettex, F. *Science and Christianity.* New York: Hodder and Stoughton, George H. Doran Co., 326 pp.

Bode, Boyd H. "The Basic Issue in Educational Theory." Unpublished paper, 1945.

Bonatti, Enrico. "The Rifting of Continents." *Scientific American* (March 1987): 97–103.

Brown, Walter T. Jr. *In the Beginning.* Naperville: Creation Research Midwest Center, 1981, 42 pp.

Clark, Gordon H. *The Philosophy of Science and Belief in God.* Nutley: The Craig Press, 1964, 95 pp.

Clark, Martin E., and Henry M. Morris. *The Bible Has the Answer.* San Diego: Creation-Life Publishers, 1976, 380 pp.

Conkin, Paul K. *American Christianity in Crisis.* Waco, Texas: Baylor University Press, 1981, 48 pp.

Deason, Gary B. "Reformation Theology and the Mechanistic Conception of Nature." *God and Nature.* Lindberg and Numbers, eds. 167–191.

De Jong, Norman, and Jack Van Der Slik. *Separation of Church and State: The Myth Revisited*. Jordan Station, Ontario: Paideia Press, 1985, 208 pp.

De Jong, Peter. "Confessing the Creator in Astronomy: A Good Guide." *The Outlook* (May 1987): pp. 6–9.

De Koster, Lester. "Review of the Fourth Day," by Howard J. Van Til. *The Outlook* (February 1987).

De Vries, John. *Beyond The Atom*. Grand Rapids: Wm. B. Eerdmans Pub. Co., 1950, 200 pp.

Draper, John William. *History of the Conflict Between Religion and Science*. New York: D. Appleton and Co., 1897.

Duncan, Homer. *Evolution: True or False*. Lubbock: MC International Publications, 1986, 25 pp.

Dundes, Alan, ed. *The Flood Myth*. Berkeley: University of California Press, 1988, 452 pp.

Durbin, Bill Jr. "How It All Began: Why Can't Evangelical Scientists Agree?" *Christianity Today* (August 12 1988): 31–40.

Evans, M. Stanton. "Evolution: a Theory in Crisis." *Christian Renewal* 5 no. 4 (October 1986): 1, 12.

Fischer, Robert B. *God Did It, but How?* La Mirada, Ca.: Cal Media, 1981, 113 pp.

Geisler, Dr. Norman L. *The Creator in the Courtroom: "Scopes II." The Controversial Arkansas Creation-Evolution Trial*. Milford: Mott Media, Inc., 1982, 242 pp.

Gieryn, Thomas F. "Boundary—Work and the Demarcation of Science from Non—Science: Strains and Interests in Professional Ideologies of Scientists." *American Sociological Review* 48 (December 1983): 781–795.

Gillispie, Charles Coulston. *Genesis and Geology*. New York: Harper and Row Publishers, 1951.

Gould, Stephen Jay. "Darwinism Defined: The Difference Between Fact and Theory." *Discover (January 1987): 64–70*.

Gould, Stephen Jay. "Evolution and the Triumph of Homology, or Why History Matters." American Scientist 74 (January, February 1986): 60–69.

Gould, Stephen Jay. "Knight Takes Bishop? The facts about the great Wilberforce-Huxley debate don't always fit the legend." *Natural History* (May 1986): 18–33.

Gregory, Frederick. "The Impact of Darwinian Evolution on Protestant Theology in the Nineteenth Century." *God and Nature*. Lindberg and Numbers, eds. 369–390.

Ham, Ken. *The Lie: Evolution*. El Cajon: Master Books, 1987, 169 pp.

Hodge, Charles. *What is Darwinism?* New York: Scribner, Armstrong and Co., 1874.

Hoffer, Eric. *The True Believer*. Mentor edition. New York: Harper and Row, 1958.

Hooykaas, R. *Religion and the Rise of Modern Science*. Grand Rapids, Mich.: William B. Eerdmans Pub. Co., 1972.

Hummel, Charles E. *The Galileo Connection: Resolving Conflicts between Science and the Bible*. InterVarsity Press, 1986, 293 pp.

Kennedy, Gail. *Evolution and Religion: The Conflict between Science and Theology in Modern America*. Boston: Heath and Co., 1957, 114 pp.

Kerr, Richard A. "Does Chaos Permeate the Solar System?" *Science* 244 (April 14, 1989): 144–145.

Langford, Jerome. *Galileo, Science and the Church*. New York: Desclee Co., 1966.

Lewin, Roger. "Statistical Traps Lurk in the Fossil Record." *Research News* 1 (May 1987): 521.

Lindberg, David C., and Ronald L. Numbers. "Beyond War and Peace: A Reappraisal of the Encounter between Christianity and Science." Unpublished paper, 1986, 27 pp.

Lindberg, David C., and Ronald L. Numbers, eds. *God and Nature: Historical Essays on the Encounter between Christianity and Science*. Berkeley: University of Calif. Press., 1986, 516 pp.

Livingstone, David N. "Evangelicals and the Darwinian Controversies." *Evangelical Studies Bulletin*. 4 no. 2 (November 1987), 12 pp.

Locke, John. "An Essay Concerning Human Understanding." in Harris, Errol E. *Fundamentals of Philosophy: A Study of Classical Texts*. New York: Holt, Rinehart and Winston, Inc., 1969.

Locke, John. *The Reasonableness of Christianity*. Ed. by I.T. Ramsey. London: Adam and Charles Block, 1958, 102 pp.

Lyell, Charles. *Principles of Geology*. 1. Hafner Service. Reprint of 1839 ed., 1970.

Maatman, Russell. "The Origins Debate, Part 2: Removing Peripheral Questions." *Pro Rege*. 16 no. 4 (June 1986): 9–19.

Mennega, Aaldert. "From Fish to Amphibian—Impossible." *The Outlook* (November 1987): 4–5.

Merton, Robert K. "Puritanism, Pietism, and Science." *The Sociological Review*. 28 no. 17 (January 1936): 1–30.

Miles, Sara Joan. "The Roots of the Scientific Revolution: Reformed Theology." *Journal of the American Scientific Affiliation*. 37 no. 3 (September 1985): 158–168.

Moore, James R. *The Post-Darwinian Controversies:* A Study of the Protestant Struggle to Come to Terms with Darwin in Great Britain and America, 1870–1900. Cambridge: Cambridge University Press, 1979.

Morgan, John. "Puritanism and Science: A Reinterpretation." *The Historical Journal*. 22 no. 3 (1979): 535–60.

Morris, Henry M., Duane T. Gish, eds. *The Battle for Creation*. Vol. 2. San Diego: Christian Life Publishers, 1976, 321 pp.

. . . . *The Biblical Basis for Modern Science*. El Cajon: Institute for Creation Research, 1989.

. . . . *The Genesis Record: A Scientific and Devotional Commentary on the Book of Beginnings*. El Cajon: Institute for Creation Research, 1989

. . . . *The Long War against God*. El Cajon: Institute for Creation Research, 1989.

. . . . *the Remarkable Record of Job*. El Cajon: Institute for Creation Research.

National Academy of Sciences. *Science and Creationism*. Washington, D.C., 1984.

Nisbet, Robert A. "A Presuppositional Approach to the Four View Model of Biological Origins." *Origins Research*. 11 no. 2 (1988): 1, 14–16.

Numbers, Ronald L. "Science and Religion." *OSIRIS*. 1 (1985): 59–80.

Parker, Gary. *Creation: The Facts of Life*. San Diego: CLP Publishers, 1980, 163 pp.

. . . . *Life before Birth*. El Cajon: Institute for Creation Research.

. . . . *Dry Bones . . . and Other Fossils*. El Cajon: Institute for Creation Research.

Patten, Donald Wesley. *The Biblical Flood and the Ice Epoch*. Grand Rapids, Mich. Baker Book House: 1966.

Pedersen, Olaf. "Galileo and the Council of Trent: The Galileo Affair Revisited." *Journal for the History of Astronomy*. 14 (1983).

Peter, Frances M. *Science and Creationalism: A View from the National Academy of Sciences*. Washington D.C.: National Academy Press, 1984, 28 pp.

Praamsma, L. *Let Christ Be King: Reflections on the Life and Times of Abraham Kuyper*. Jordan Station, Ontario: Paideia Press, 1985, 196 pp.

Ratzsch, Del. *Philosophy of Science: The Natural Sciences in Christian Perspective*. Downers Grove: InterVarsity Press, 1986, 165 pp.

Ross, Hugh. "Cosmology Confronts the Creator." *Origins Research*. 10 no. 2 (1987): 1–2.

Rudwick, Martin. "Senses of the Natural World and Senses of God: Another Look at the Historical Relation of Science and Religion." *The Sciences and Theology in the Twentieth Century,* edited by A. R. Peacocke. South Bend: Notre Dame Univiversity Press, 1981, pp. 241–261.

Shelton, John S. *Geology Illustrated*. San Francisco: W. H. Freeman and Co., 1966.

Siemens, David F. "Six Days, Six Ages, or . . . ?" *Journal of the American Scientific Affiliation* 38, no. 2 (June 1986): 128–131.

Turner, Frank M. "The Victorian Conflict between Science and Religion: A Professional Dimension." *ISIS* 69 no. 248 (1978): 356–376.

Shipman, Pat. "A Culture Divided by Science." *Education Week* 6 no. 4 (October 1, 1986).

Van Til, Howard J., Davis A. Young, Clarence Menninga. *Science Held Hostage*. Downers Grove: InterVarsity Press, 1988, 189 pp.

Van Til, Howard J. *The Fourth Day: What the Bible and the Heavens Are Telling Us about the Creation*. Grand Rapids: Wm. B. Eerdmans Pub. Co., 1986.

Vos, Johannes G. "The Bearing of Scriptural Revelation on the Evolutionary World View." *The Outlook* (April 1987): 20–22.

Waltke, Bruce. "The First Seven Days." *Christianity Today* (August 12, 1988): 42–46.

Weinberg, Alvin M. "How the Scientific Marketplace Works." *International Journal on the Unity of the Sciences* 1 no. 4 (1988): 377–386.

Westfall, Richard S. "The Rise of Science and the Decline of Orthodox Christianity: A Study of Kepler, Descartes, and Newton." *God and Nature*. Lindberg and Numbers eds. 218–237.

Whitcomb, John C., and Henry M. Morris. *The Genesis Flood: The Biblical Record and Its Scientific Implications*. Grand Rapids: Baker Book House, 1962.

White, Andrew Dickson. *A History of the Warfare of Science with Theology*. Two volumes. New York: Dover Publications, Inc., 1896. (Dover Edition, pub. 1960.)

Wolterstorff, Nicholas. *Curriculum: By What Standard?* Grand Rapids: National Union of Christian Schools, 1976.

Wolterstroff, Nicholas. *Reason within the Bounds of Religion*. 2nd ed., Grand Rapids: Eerdmans Pub. Co., 1976. 161 pp.

Young, Davis A. *Christianity and the Age of the Earth*. Grand Rapids: Zondervan Pub. Co., 1982.

Young, E. J. *In the Beginning*. Edinburgh: Banner of Truth Trust, 1976, 117 pp.

Index

a priori commitments, 77
Abraham, birth of 45, 46, 47
Adam, birth of, 20, 45, 46
Agassiz, Louis, 11, 31, 66-69, 73-76, 82, 84
Age of Enlightenment 30, 67, 74
Age of Science, 25, 75, 80, 84
Alps, 66, 67
American Scientific Affiliation, 5
antithesis, 14, 18, 38, 44
Aquinas, Thomas, 13
Arkansas, Balanced Treatment Act, 4
atom, 15

Bailyn, Bernard, 34
Belgic, 41
Beyond the Atom, 15
"Big Bang" theory, 37, 85
Bishop Usher, 39
bride, 17, 57
bridegroom, 57
British Association for the Advancement of Science 10
Buckland, William, 67

Calvin College, 7
Calvin, John, 13, 15, 71, 74, 78, 81
Canadian Rockies, 67
Censorship: Evidence of Bias in our Children's Textbooks, 34
Christ, as the Bridegroom, 57
Christian College coalition, 1
Christian education (schools), 34, 37
Christian Renewal, 71, 72, 73, 74, 78, 82, 83, 84
Church, as the Bride of Christ, 17, 57
conflict, 11
conformity, 5

constitution of the U.S., 34
Copernicus, Nicolaus, 12
covenant, 56, 57

Darwin, Charles, 10, 15, 31, 59, 67
dating, 39, 47, 48, 50, 51, 52,
day, meaning of, 39, 40, 41, 42, 44
De Vries, John, 15, 16
Death Valley, 76
Draper, John William, 11, 17, 18
Dundes, Alan, 50

eschatology, 51
Etudes sue les Glaciers (Studies on Glaciers), 66

Falsehood, definition of, 4, 5, 22
flood, Noahic, 31, 36, 45, 50, 56, 57, 65, 66, 68, 72, 73, 74, 77, 81, 82, 83
fossils, 26, 29, 50, 69, 83

Galileo affair, 7, 12
Geology Illustrated, 71, 73, 74, 84
glacial epoch theory, 66, 67, 68, 73, 77, 82, 84
glaciation, 66, 72, 80, 85
Glacier National Park, 67, 83
Gould, Stephen, 51, 59
Grand Canyon, 9, 63
Great Basin, 62, 76, 79, 84
Great Salt Lake, 76, 84

Harvard University, 66
Hegel, Georg Friedrich, 14
History of the Conflict Between Religion and Science, 11
History of the Warfare of Science with Theology in Christendom, 8, 10, 11, 17, 20, 26, 33, 82

Hodge, Charles, 11, 12, 27
Huxley, Thomas Henry, 10, 12

Ice Age theory, 31, 44, 65, 66, 69, 76, 79

Job, 52, 53

Kant, Immanuel, 13
Keplar, Johannes, 12
Kettle Moraine State Park, 67
knowledge, 3, 17, 27, 32, 69
Knox, John, 13

Lewis, C.S., 21
Lindberg, David, 12, 27
Lobbes, J.C., 15
Luther, Martin, 4, 13
Lyell, Charles, 31, 50, 61, 67, 69, 85

Mann, Horace, 38
Massachusetts Board of Education, 38
Mead, Sidney, 33, 34
Menninga, Clarence, 65, 72, 73, 78, 81
metaphor, 7, 11, 12, 14
Museum of Natural History, 68, 84
myth, 51

National Academy of Sciences, 4, 6
National Science Foundation, 5
neutrality, 15, 34, 35, 36, 37, 38
Newton, Isaac, 12
Niagara Falls, 67, 68, 83
Noahic flood, date of, 44, 46, 52, 67, 69, 83
Numbers, Ronald L., 1, 2, 12

ocean trenches, 84, 85
Onward Christian Soldiers, 10, 21
Origin of Species, 10, 15, 21, 31, 60, 67

Pleistocene Age, 62, 76, 77
Principles of Geology, 31, 52, 68, 85
proof, definition of, 67, 69, 76

rainbow, 55, 56, 57, 58

Sagan, Carl, 48, 51, 59
Satan, 17, 20, 21, 22, 23, 29, 47
Science Held Hostage, 0, 13
science, as method, 25, 28
science, definition of, 28
scientific method, 2, 6, 26, 27, 28, 51, 69, 76, 77
scientism, 31, 32
scientist's, 35
scientist, 14, 20, 25, 27, 35, 46, 76
Scopes Trial, 7
Scripture, authority of, 12
Scripture, Christocentric character of, 46
Sea of Illinois, 69
separation of church and state, 5, 34
Shelton, John S., 61, 71, 73, 74, 75, 76, 77, 84
"Soapy Sam" (Wilberforce), 10, 11, 12
Stowe, Hariet Beecher, 4
Switzerland, 37, 67

The Flood Myth, 50
The Fourth Day, 13, 35, 36, 48, 69
The Origin of Species, 10, 15, 21, 31, 60, 67
theistic evolution, 5, 7, 8, 9, 13, 14, 18, 29, 38, 59
turf wars, 29, 30

uniformitarianism, 30, 50, 68, 76

Van Til, Howard, 6, 35, 36, 48, 49, 59, 69, 74
Vitz, Paul, 34

warfare metaphor, 7, 11, 12, 14
Westminster Confession, 8, 41, 83
Whewell, Rev. Wm., 27
White, Andrew Dickson, 11, 12, 17, 18
White's, 11
Wilberforce, "Soapy Sam", 10, 11, 12
Wisconsin, 66, 67, 68, 72, 81
Wolterstorff, Nicholas, 35